My Hands held out to You

GIANCARLO MORONI

# MY HANDS HELD OUT TO YOU

The Use of Body and
Hands in Prayer

Translated from the Italian by Paul Burns

**PAULIST PRESS**
New York · Mahwah

Published in the USA by
Paulist Press
997 Macarthur Boulevard
Mahwah, NJ 07430

Published originally in Italy by Editrice Queriniana, Brescia, under
the title *Le Mie Mani verso Te*, in 1989

Original edition © Editrice Queriniana, Brescia 1989

English translation © Burns & Oates/Search Press Ltd 1992

ISBN: 0-8091-3328-8

Printed in Great Britain

# Contents

# PART ONE
# BODY

# 1
# WHY THE "BODY"?

Defining our body means defining us as human beings. Today especially, so many of us are trying to understand what lies within us, and to seek out a truer, more authentic way of *communicating through our lives.*

Physical science teaches us that our bodily reality forms the primitive and original structural space that fleshes out our presence in the world. The first thing we have to do is look beyond the dualism that separates matter from spirit, the physical from the psychic. **The human person is one and indivisible.**

Ancient philosophy, especially Greek, has for centuries conditioned theological and pastoral thinking, giving the body a negative image.

There have also been frequent attempts to justify this negative view of the body by recourse to the scriptures. These overlook the fact that the body is seen *as the person* in his/her outward and visible aspect (see Rom. 6:12, 12:1), to the point where the term can be used as a personal pronoun (compare 1 Cor. 6:19 and 3:17, or 1 Cor. 6:15 and Eph. 5:30). These attempts also place excessive stress on the symbol of *flesh* used to specify our earthly and fragile condition.

What is true is that, "without casting doubt on the dignity of the body, Paul puts forward his own theology of it. *Flesh,* indwelt by *sin,* has enslaved the *body* (meaning: the person). Now there is a *sinful body,* because sin can

9

dominate the body and this can lead to death (Rom. 7:24). The body, then, is identified with flesh in its harmful sense (Rom. 6:12, 8:13), and designates the human person enslaved to sin" (Xavier Léon-Dufour, *Dictionary of the New Testament*).

This is a theology peculiar to Paul, but of course by no means exhausts the complexity of his theology. Suffice to read 1 Corinthians 12:12–27 to be drawn into the exaltation of the human body as a concrete, tangible symbol of the reality of the *mystical **Body of Christ**!* For too long, however, we have tended to limit ourselves to just one aspect of this image, and if this is made the only one, then we risk being left with a distorted view of the reality. In effect, the Bible uses "body" to mean, above all, that with which we enter into relation with others and with the universe, and which therefore constitutes our sole possibility of communicating, of expressing ourselves. So: **the body is the person expressing him/herself in visible form**; it is the outward manifestation of our inner bearing. This is why the body can still indicate the human person enslaved to sin.

In Jesus Christ, however, the *body of flesh* is the visible place where the intimate and invisible reconciliation between humankind and the Father takes place.

This symbolism not only allows us to reflect on the body, and – in this book – on our hands in particular, but *assures us of the legitimacy of doing so*: recourse to the scriptures uncovers a discourse rich in bodily symbols and analogies that, while on the one hand showing God's deep pedagogical concern in the use of simple *words* that we can understand to communicate profound truths, on the other allows us to be drawn into the expressive potentiality of our bodies, capable of putting us in contact not only with our fellows and with nature, but also with the very God, in community and individual *liturgy*.

In what follows I will briefly set out a reflection on the

"body" phenomenon, indicating what has been said about it at various stages of the history of philosophy, theology and culture. I will then try to focus attention on a particular part of our body: *our hands*. These will be the subject of detailed observations, both from a cultural-emotive point of view and from a biblical one. This stage will lead us to a deeper examination of the expressive capabilities of our hands and their power in communicating through their symbolic language, both in ordinary human and in religious dialogue. This deeper understanding is approached through practical exercises, which can be carried out in groups or individually, in the privacy of one's own room. The particular consideration given here to *hands* could (and should) be the first stage in a process of interiorization, leading on to consider other parts of our bodies that are particularly rich in symbolic meaning, both in our day-to-day lives and in our relations with God, as revealed to us in the Bible.

# 2
# BODY AND . . . SOUL

Our *bodies* are the great discovery that men and women make in their growth process, and also the reality that requires an ever renewed understanding of how they are an expression of the *whole person*.

Accepting our body, formed as it is, defining us as men or women in relation to nature, society and God, is the characteristic element without which we can never take our life in hand and live it.

The body, besides all the active and passive conditionings it can bring into being, allows human beings to express themselves at all levels.

It is our body that allows us to situate ourselves as men and women in the history of the human race, in which we are all, each in our own way, called to take a place.

It is my body, as it is formed and sexed, that puts my person in relation to that part of humankind which is other than me, and which I must try to meet and accept in serenity, balance and harmony.

It is, precisely, through my body that I express my being and it is again thanks to my body that I am able to enter into creative and productive relationships with everything that is outside me. Thanks to my body, and accepting all its limitations and qualities, I can enter into relationships with others to the extent that they manifest their bodies to me with all their limitations and qualities.

Each of us, young or old, at every stage of interiorizing

12

our own experience, should feel called to take on, seriously and responsibly, the task of building up, not only our own personality, but also, together with others, a freer humankind. Turning our backs on this task would mean running the risk of disorientation and loneliness. Our body, with the numerous changes through which it goes, places us in a constant state of uncertainty and quest for new ways of behaving. It is in such moments that we all feel drawn to the multiplicity of models which society presents to us through the mass media.

Even those who have found a measure of stability in their behaviour are liable, at times of change, to give way to the feelings of unease that beset them and disturb their conscience.

Perhaps there is a way that leads human beings to live freely, and perhaps this might be *discovering the joy of "being" in a body*. This is a joy that leads to a freeing of one's feelings, to a realization of one's dreams and desires, while respecting the dreams and desires of others around one.

This is an experience that no one can ask another person to make for one, or make for another person. We each have to find out for ourselves what it is that unites us to or divides us from external reality and other people. And this experience allows us to make another discovery – that joy is like a spark leaping between persons immersed in a climate of reciprocal and unconditioned acceptance of their own being and that of other people.

Each of us will then have the delightful surprise of discovering that:

* accepting one's own body means accepting life, accepting living in a well-defined situation as a woman or a man;
* accepting one's own body with its sexual characteristics means accepting that one has need of other people in order to be a balanced, harmonious and complete person;

* accepting one's own body means accepting entering into relationships with others.

All this can be obtained by consenting to live our own human experience:

   – attentive to what happens around us;
   – with courage, freeing ourselves from all fears;
   – with patience, without making claims on other people;
   – in the conviction that it is up to us, at all times, to find the proper response;
   – with openness, eliminating all self-absorption and all individualism;
   – being prepared to take risks, not closing ourselves off through prejudice;
   – with serenity, without anguish or discouragement;
   – in dialogue, listening and meeting;
   – with sincerity, without hiding things or hiding anything from ourselves;
   – with constancy, without letting ourselves be overcome by difficulties and without taking refuge in surrogates or just "what we like";
   – knowing how to find enough time for things that matter;
   – in total acceptance of ourselves, without evasions, mystifications, sublimations and fantastic dreams.

## Overcoming Dualism and the Quest for Personal Unity

"Religious" attitudes toward the body are, naturally, tinged with a moral view linked above all to those manifestations of life that concern sexuality and thereby strongly condition our culture.

Today any expedient is sought to succeed in liberating us from this conception. Perhaps the dominant concern is to recover the value of the body as an active and irreplacable collaborator in personal development.

This *human* quest for a revaluation of the body seems to be in harmony with the concepts introduced into Western culture at the outset of Christianity by theological reflection on the **incarnation of the Son of God**.

Different philosophical currents, too, have contributed to this thrust toward *liberation*, sometimes in opposition to, sometimes in support of the theological view. So it seems useful to set out some elements of the question of the body as it has been approached in the history of thought. From this will emerge the classic relationship with the soul and with religious morality.

One prior observation needs to be made:
Human beings display extremely complex physical and psychic characteristics and functions, which are therefore difficult to analyze and reduce to a synthesis.

How the body is viewed, then, depends on the interpretation made of what human beings are.

According to some (Nietzsche, for one), the body is the element that defines human beings, while the functions attributed to the soul are subsumed into the body itself.

According to others (such as Plato), the essential human element is the soul, while the body plays an altogether subordinate role.

According to yet others (Aristotle, for example), human beings are a synthesis between body and soul.

Depending on whether the body is seen as a spiritual or material reality, as homogeneous or heterogeneous with respect to the soul, differing concepts will emerge, viewing human beings themselves either as a basic unity or as made up of two constituent parts.

The problem of the unity of human beings has major implications for the subject of their survival after death –

more specifically, for the question of the immortality of the soul.

*Platonic dualism,* which in certain respects goes back beyond Plato, is the concept that has had the deepest influence on Western culture. **Plato** saw the body as the seat of the soul, but judged it as the *tomb* or *prison* of the soul itself, in that the soul participates in the *stable* world of ideas, to which it aspires to be united, while the body, in a state of *becoming,* exposed to decomposition, and being of a different nature, is more of a hindrance than anything else. This concept, developed in various ways, has led to what is known as *contempt for the body.*

**Aristotle** reacted to Plato by stressing the unity of the person: the body is an instrument – the image used is that of an axe in the hands of a woodcutter. The soul, in this image, is what moves the axe to chop. So the whole person can be re-defined as an *axe that chops*: this would be a unity made up of elements that can be picked out and distinguished. Aristotle, however, is ambiguous on the possibility of the soul being separated from the body.

Dualism had a profound influence on the **Middle Ages**, and later. It can be seen obviously in **Descartes**, who saw the person as made up of *res cognitans*, the spirit, and of *res extensa*, matter, both components being perfectly separable. Without meaning to, Descartes thereby prepared the ground for a materialist viewpoint: the separability of the body is, in effect, the condition for its *complete autonomy.*

In more recent times, **idealism** – as propounded by **Schelling** and **Hegel** – by going beyond the spiritual dualism that makes up much of modern philosophy, set out the premises for a renewed unitary consideration of the human person. For Hegel, the body is dialectically incorporated in a process whose absolute protagonist is the spirit. The body is merely a *sign* of the spirit, which cannot dissociate itself from the natural "accidents" that characterize the body, but which must necessarily pursue its own course till it reaches its full development in philosophy.

A **unitary** concept of the person is found, first, in the **school of Hegel**, which developed materialist theses in reaction against Hegel's theology and abstractionism, and later in **Nietzsche**, who proclaimed that the *human person coincides with the body.*

Closer to our day, **phenomenology** and **existentialism** have insistently drawn attention to the body. **Husserl**, regarded as the father of phenomenology, stressed the need to develop a strict science that could subsist once all traditional scientific constructs and even the generally accepted modes of thought had been set aside. Once all these particular conditionings had been removed, Husserl concentrated on the intentionality of pure knowledge, that is, the direct contact between subject and object that can be established on such premises: *the phenomenon* (= what is apparent) *is the very manifestation of reality.* **Merleau-Ponty**, generally included in the phenomenological current, but extremely sensitive to existentialist discourse, interpreted phenomenological discourse in a sense that placed the body centre stage.

For him, the body is the place in which the world is constituted for the subject: on one hand it belongs to the world, and can be measured with the instruments of science (anatomy, physiology, biology, physics, chemistry, etc.); on the other, it expresses the particular viewpoint of the subject. Merleau-Ponty insists on the indissociability of these two aspects that place human perception in a radical ambiguity: this in effect expresses both anonymous and impersonal objectivity, and the presence of the subject to him/herself. One aspect can never be reduced to the other. In *The Phenomenology of Perception*, he wrote: "The body is not an object, but is that through which we view objects"; and: "The body is the vehicle of our being in the world, and for a living being having a body means being tied to a definite environment, caught up in certain projects and continually struggling."

Knowledge is "the thing being inherent by means of the body." "The body is our normal manner of having a world; sometimes this is limited to actions necessary for the preservation of life and correlatively places a biological world around us; sometimes, using these first actions and moving from their actual meaning to a figurative meaning, it manifests through them a nucleus of new significance. This is the case with habitual movements such as dance. Sometimes, finally, the significance sought cannot be attained through natural human means, and it then needs to be formed into an instrument (language, for example) and to project a cultural world around itself."

These, then, are the various ways in which bodily experience has been seen, and so the ways in which we have continually documented our being situated in the world.

In **contemporary culture**, not just in philosophy, the attention paid to the body, encouraged by the ever more analytical studies undertaken by various disciplines, such as biology, psychology and psychoanalysis, has perhaps led to *the person being reduced to his/her body*, in the sense that the whole complex of meanings that were posited of the whole human being have come to converge on the body. In general, however, this means concentrating on the unity of the whole human being: the body is no longer seen as a disposable appendage, but as an essential point of reference in understanding basic human behaviour.

# 3
# THE BODY IN CONTEMPORARY CULTURE

In our Western culture, dominated, as I have suggested above, by the theological vision of the *incarnation of the Son of God in Jesus of Nazareth,* the role taken on by the *human body* can appear all the more strange.

This reality, this complex and marvellous mode of being, which for us constitutes the only manner offered to us of living out our earthly experience, as persons, has had to adapt itself to the most bizarre modes of usage, of exploitation, of exaltation and of rejection, of which only the human *mind* is capable.

Every stage of our Western culture has seen in the body either the image of creativity or the spectre of anguish.

Human beings, by their nature, are *in solidarity with* the Absolute, with God, with whom they share the powers of *understanding* (from *intus-legere* = reading within reality), *will (as the expression of freedom of choice among values discovered) and love* (as communication of self to another in acceptance of that other).

But our bodily, material reality imposes another form of *solidarity* on us: with the cosmos; that is, with nature. Our body, for good or ill, is the element that *limits* our capacity by reason of its dependence on the physical laws of space and time; that is, the dimensions that determine the *environment* in which all material reality is born, develops and dies.

Now, depending on the predominance in a given

19

culture of one or other solidarity, the body will be seen as: either, an element of balance, capable of sharing the power to put the capabilities that liken us to God into action; or, simply as a *misfortune, a burden* to be carried, and, therefore, to be mortified, to be rendered ever more innocuous, since it is the cause of all human ills.

## Characteristics of the Body in Contemporary Culture

At all times, our concept of the body has been linked to the status it has assumed in art, religion, and politics. Contemporary culture seems also to be subject to the same laws.

All the same, contrary to what might be thought, there does not seem to be the same concern to seek a synthesis between the two human solidarities – a synthesis that has always been present in the culture and philosophy of the East, of India especially, finding its greatest expression in *yoga*, which means precisely the *integration, the wholeness* of human bodily and spiritual reality.

For us in the West today, the body is conceived as how human beings project, communicate, *tell themselves*. Hence the quest for ever new forms of making the body *its own author*, in the sense of being capable of arousing feelings, rather than making emotions live.

Rather than a synthesis of the Platonic dichotomy, which so influenced earlier cultural expressions, today we seek a way beyond this intellectual wrangle by providing the body alone with the possibility of being, in itself and for itself, the source of aesthetic pleasure, of *hedonism*. And this expression seems to coincide exactly with the need for human beings today to be *persons*.

## How the Body has changed, and why

In recent years our body has undergone radical changes: it has become more demanding. There is a continual need to find new fashions, new images, new looks. But above all, it seems to have acquired the requirement of *freedom*. It wants to be free to speak, to act, to demonstrate, to represent, to tell. No road should be closed to it, no experience denied it, in every field from cinema and theatre to dance, video, fashion.

The great protagonists of this change are, naturally, the *idols* of sport, the screen, music. In reality, however, these are merely models, examples from which this new *body consciousness* seeks inspiration.

The real *heroes* are the mass of the people who use their bodies every day: the muscle-men on club doors, the tireless housewives following aerobics on video, not to mention the Saturday-night ballerinas of the discos.

What can motivate such a revolution, inspire people to persist in this marathon leading to the achievement of a new physical image, a new concept of the body?

By now, the need to overcome the dichotomy, the rupture prevalent in earlier cultures between *intellectual body* and *animal body*, is widespread and established. This rupture basically caused people to distance themselves from the *animal body* and its needs for whole generations, and its effects were plain to see. And they can still be seen today, present above all in the difficulty we have in understanding the language of the body, its messages and requests.

Today a great revolution is taking place: people are rediscovering the body, and doing so of their own free will, with no pressure from obligation or competition. The first symptom of this genuine basic discovery is the massive participation in non-competitive sports and leisure activities. A real transformation is happening, a real taking stock, a real understanding of the body's needs by an ever-growing number of people.

In this revolution, cultural and socio-economic differences do not matter; what exist are possibilities or impossibilities of being concerned with one's own body in relation to existing or non-existing structures, and also in relation to anyone who can educate, provide an example, create a culture. All that is needed is someone to help people project their image of themselves: many of us have so much inside us, but are very inhibited and dare not allow it to come out. We lack the means to take possession of and manipulate the expressive capabilities locked inside our bodies.

This new culture is deeply convinced that all we have to do is *train*, sensitize our own bodies, appreciate the beauty of our own musculature, in order to feel good . . . *in our own skin*! Sexuality itself derives its communicative charge from the fact that we feel good in ourselves. When we feel well physically, we are happy with our appearance, with the way we feel, with the image of ourselves we convey to others, and . . . we are pleased with ourselves.

The current tendency to want to show ourselves off, to exhibit the image of our body at all costs, may seem to be the fruit of an excessively superficial need, or of a pathological quest for self-image. But the motives arise, rather, from deeper needs, and also from the fact of having rediscovered the pleasure of being able to heal one's *self*, of *self-improvement*.

The body, in the past, was the great absentee, the great stranger or great demon: it was, therefore, either repressed or exalted. Now, however, we are looking for the happy mean: a comfortable relationship with ourselves.

But in this quest, we run the risk of moving toward a body that is more and more *image*, an ever-greater *spectacle*, ever more desirous of achieving a *look* of its own, a way of appearing covered in *signals* that reveal the *identikit* of the *self* of any one of us. A body on which we can trace designs and decorations, which we can make into a rainbow of colour. A body in which there will be a huge space for sensations, and also a little space for emotions, even if they are only minor emotions.

## How this New Image of the Body has Developed

This revolution in body-image has been carried out according to specific rules. Massive contributions have been made by the cinema, the theatre, dance, television and fashion. The widest expression of the quest is certainly through *dance*, in all its technical variety and folkloric forms, from classical ballet through folk dance and rock to flash and break . . . . In modern dance, the attitudes expressed often become a sublimation of violence: instead of taking knives to one another, we dance at each other! Schools of dance multiply and are ever more widely attended, especially since dancing has taken on a therapeutic quality not only for the body, but also for the inner person, for the *spirit*. It is, in fact, claimed that: *dancing helps one to know one's own body so as to be better able to relate to the "great body" that is the world.*

In the theatre, too, the body has been, and, particularly since the 1970s, is, the great protagonist: a theatre of gesture, not, therefore, so dependent on the script, on words, on dialogue, as on pure bodily expressiveness.

The body has become a spectacle: action takes precedence over representation. A body seen not so much as project or result, but as *medium*, as the means through which an energetic flux of liberation, of contact with the audience too, must pass. A body which is involved, in all its parts, in a perfect and synchronous control of all its elements. It is in all ways an expressive unit capable of fusing all the elements of the spectacle together: from mimicry to recitation, music, song.

## A Body for Pleasing and Feeling Free

Under these pressing stimuli, widely diffused by the social

communications media, ever-greater numbers of people are discovering not just the pleasure of possessing a body in good health, but also the wish to use their bodies to **please and be pleased**, or rather, to *please through being pleased*.

Bodily fashions have succeeded one another at dizzying speeds, especially in the last few years (the main expression undoubtedly being aerobic gymnastics). The quest involved in these *fashions* is concerned with drawing together the most highly perfected techniques for having a more perfect body and living better. People who for so long were conscious of having a body only in times of sickness, and so used not to attaching much importance to it, feel, now that they have rediscovered its role, the need to take advantage of it in a hurry: they want a body they can use with pleasure and freedom.

And now gymnasia devoted to "body-building" proliferate. This technique claims to be able to build a body piece by piece, muscle by muscle, like a multi-storey building: the body is just material for modelling; creating a beautiful body has become an art form. (The whole of classical art in fact exalted the shape of the human body as the most perfect form in nature.) Men and women submit themselves to continual efforts to force their bodies to take on the appearance of a perfect, docile, domesticated machine. The *new divinity* worshipped in these heroes is in fact the body, a sculpted body, the outer image of a self-generating and self-satisfying power.

In the cinema, the body has always been a primary element: a body exhibited in public, a body as wrapper, illusion, deceit . . . .

The construction of this body has, in general, been executed outside the cinema. This has done no more than take advantage of it. In recent years above all, the cinema has dealt in bodies that fascinate, but that are also exposed to torture, to terrible trials, to transformations that lead them to *lose their identity, their image* built up at the cost of lengthy research and enormous efforts (suffice to think of those horror movies that have such wide audience appeal). The body is an *object* that can be subjected to every sort of transmogrification.

Naturally all these efforts determine a particular vision of how to build up or plan the body-image that will allow us to recognize ourselves, express ourselves, communicate what makes us what we are and accept what is presented to us by the outside world. The great challenge facing us now is to know how to discern whether this body-image is truly the most suitable means of expressing sensations and emotions, and whether the language it uses is really the most appropriate and comprehensible one. It will then, perhaps, be possible to distinguish whether contemporary culture has paid more attention to the *clothing*, to the *frame* of our body-image, than to its true essence.

But is it possible to pick out one particular responsible agent, one reason why the quest has evolved in such a dangerous and, sometimes, de-personalizing direction?

## A "Religion" and a "Theology" of the Body?

Christianity, both in its theological reflection and in its religious practices (liturgical expression, above all), has in the course of its history had an excessively cerebral view of human beings in relation to nature, **and, consequently, in their capacity to** *humanize* matter through transforming work. Centralizing human activity on our speculative capacity, our reason, has progressively reduced us to considering our own bodies as a *potentiality* from which we need to be defended, rather than something to be appreciated. That Christianity which, above all in its Western embodiment, spent much of its course under the impulse of a God who became *flesh*, today looks to contemporary eyes like an *enemy of humankind*. Holding out the promise of *future happiness*, it does not allow us to enjoy the *happiness of having a body*.

It is perhaps this reading of Christianity that has unleashed the revolution whose manifestations we have been examining. But, as in all revolutions, the way solutions are sought has pushed the problem too far in the opposite direction: Has the body been so long suffocated by religion? Well, then, now we need a *religion of the body*. Has Christian theology forgotten the incarnation of God? Right: now *flesh, the body, will be made into god* and given an adequate *theological* reflection to smile on it. Christians condemn this as materialism and hedonism, but is it right to eliminate reflection on such a central problem, simply by labelling it, or by setting limits to its vision of humankind? When all is said and done, has the vision of historical Christianity not been limited in its own theological reflection, religious practices and liturgy?

Faced, then, with these challenges – those of past and present history, those of reason and materialism – , would it not be of positive benefit to try and see if we actually do possess that unity which the Old Testament expresses as *body-soul-spirit* and which the New Testament defines as *person*, the unbreakable union of bodily and spiritual dimensions?

This could, perhaps, be the road leading us beyond the two extremes: seeing ourselves as *image* of God only in our spiritual dimension on the one hand; on the other, being in full solidarity with nature only in our bodily dimension. This, in my view, is the base on which to rest religious practice and its liturgical expression: a body charged with its own symbolic language and capable of putting us in touch not only with nature, but also with God, and doing this precisely in the very celebration God makes of himself: the eucharistic prayer.

# 4
# THE "RELIGIOUS" DIMENSION OF THE BODY

The quest to give the body value, undertaken by our contemporary "culture," would emerge as rather limited and even deviant if it were absolutized as *unique and perfect*. The line of enquiry followed in these pages, even though it does not minimize the reality of a *mortified body* for long periods of human history, is based on the attempt to draw a balanced conception from precisely those biblical writings accused of being the cause of this "mortification."

In general one is led to have recourse to the bases and practices of Eastern philosophy and religions in order to legitimize – in our Western and Christian environment too – enquiry into the role the body should play in human relationship with God, particularly in prayer.

The body, independently of religions or philosophy, has always shown itself to be indispensable in any process of communication. This prerogative of the body finds special confirmation precisely in the experience of the Hebrew people and of the early church. There is abundant documentation of this in the scriptures. The body is shown as the reality in which God's face is shown, but also as the image of humankind displaying the deformations sustained in compromise with sin.

If this second aspect has predominated in the course of history – which it would seem to have done – so as to reduce the body to a manifestation of evil or cause of estrangement from God, in the liturgy the body has never lost its centrality as the vehicle of our entering into relationship with God. Bodily symbols, in fact, form the basis of liturgical action and the celebration of the sacraments.

The only problem is that these symbols and this bodily language use a code and signs that are difficult to understand, or not perfectly in tune with our outlook today.

This leads to the justification for having recourse to Eastern religious experience to support our enquiry. It can help us to discover the roots of an experience common to us all in our efforts to enter into a relationship with God. Perhaps even we, culturally "developed" Westerners, will then be able to understand that *communication with God is made through the whole human person*, and not only on the cerebral level, let alone on the emotional level.

## Body as Relationship

The first step in this enquiry consists of being convinced that I cannot communicate with anyone if I do not first know that I am I, if I do not know how to recognize myself in my expressive capacity, and that I cannot accept anyone if I do not first know how to be *silent*, if I have not created a suitable, tranquil, welcoming space within me, if I have not first created a *void* within me. When we speak of our body, we must absolutely avoid thinking of it as a *thing*, one thing among so many others, a thing to be used. My body is not a thing! My body is esentially a relationship, it is what allows me to form a relationship with things, with the world, with time and space.

Of course: from one point of view it is and always will be a *thing*. In what sense? In the sense that it can be knocked down by a car in the street, struck by a bullet, immobilized by cancer. Nevertheless: knocked down, struck, immobilized, it is always a human body that is knocked down, struck, immobilized: *a relationship with the world has been destroyed.* This woman, this man . . . knocked down, struck, immobilized, will no longer have a relationship with their children, their spouse, their friends. *A relationship with the world is shut off, finished.* A thing, then, but a *thing of an absolutely special kind.*

My body is that reality through whose power I am inserted into this world; it is the reality that allows me to form relationships with the infinitely little and the infinitely great.

Thanks to our bodies, we are an integral part of the whole world, and, therefore, the world is a constituent part of our bodies. And Christ too, *through the incarnation in Jesus of Nazareth*, comes to be part of our world. But he comes into it to transform it, to transfigure it, to dissolve this "body of dust" and usher in a *new relationship* with the divine.

## Body as Image to Build

This body, this relationship with things, the world and God, is not something *already made*, pre-formed. It is a reality to be built, to be continually updated, and, above all, to re-cognize and, in this, to re-cognize itself and, through this, to be re-cognized.

We have already seen that building this image is a very widespread concern. The cult of the body: how to develop it, how to improve its powers of communication, how to beautify it, how to make it a docile instrument for giving and receiving pleasure . . . .

For believers too, and therefore from a religious point of view, this body needs to recover its image in order to be capable of revealing and communicating the image of God that dwells in us.

My appearance is born and develops gradually as I risk

making it say exactly what I want: when through it I can communicate, be and display what I try and what I desire. Of course there is no question of reaching this point from one day to the next: a long preparation is needed, a punctilious apprenticeship carried out in uncertainties and fresh starts, a respectful *obedience* to the feelings of my heart and the demands of my will.

The adult embodiment of this image is that capable of expressing what I wish, at the exact monent, in the right place, and in the most appropriate manner. This will be an image very like that of "freedom." Such an image is one step from the internal reality of the "I" of the person displaying it. The sign of the maturity of this image (*not achieved all at once, but constantly brought up to date*) will be seen when we can sincerely say: "This is my body! This is my face! This is me defining myself!"

In practice, however, we realize that our experience of our body, as we know it, is charged with problems. In effect, we are up against a double limitation:

* first, we have to cope with *matter and its laws*. For all our deeds and endeavours, we shall never achieve a perfect harmony. Our body can never be the perfect expression of what we wish to communicate; it will always be something of an obstacle. Its outward appearance translates our thought, but may also betray it – "*traduttore, traditore,*" as the Italians say!
* second, we are liable to sin. This, in effect, is what breaks our relationship with others. Just as the body is no longer a body if it is prevented from being in contact with others, so it can itself become an instrument of shutting out, of isolation.

## Jesus as Image of the Risen Body

A risen person is not someone freed from the body, but set free from all the weaknesses of the body and the obstacles it presented. **The risen one is someone for whom the body is finally body: that is, that reality through whose power he expresses himself, loves, performs.** We simply have to change our way of thinking about it.

We have always thought of the risen body in relation to our actual bodies. Now, on the other hand, we can understand our actual bodies in relation to the risen body of Jesus. Our mortal bodies are just a *sketch*, a *design* which has a promised fulfillment, a finished work of art.

> *He is the image of the unseen God,*
> *the first born of all creation . . .*
> *And he is the head of his body, the church;*
> *he is the beginning*
> *and was first raised from the dead . . .*
> *So then, if you are risen with Christ,*
> *seek the things that are above* (Col. 1:15, 18; 3:1).

> *For us, our citizenship is in heaven,*
> *where we await the coming of our Saviour,*
> *Jesus Christ, the Lord.*
> *He will transfigure our lowly body,*
> *making it like his own body, radiant in glory,*
> *through the power that is his*
> *to submit everything to himself* (Phil. 3:20–21).

However, we all know that *"the things that are above"* have to be seen now from *"here below."* *"Our citizenship"* (the reign of God) has to be prepared by us on this earth, by living it and preparing ourselves to live it in its fullness. In reality, this means building our image at every step of our lives so that it can reveal that of God.

To reach this point we have to make the body we *have* tally with the body we *are*, through the various transformations required of us by life itself. The caterpillar has to leave its caterpillar body to take on that of the butterfly: it has to die to its *image* of caterpillar to assume the *imago* of butterfly. The death of the first is the indispensable condition for the life of the second.

Jesus himself, almost as though to announce his transformation, likened himself to a *grain of wheat: "Unless the grain of wheat falls to the earth and dies, it remains alone; but if it dies, it produces much fruit"* (John 12:24).

It is easy to allow ourselves to believe that we are nothing more than "the body we *have*": we see this as our only source of pleasure thanks to the knowledge it provides us with, the emotions it emits, the sensations it perceives. It is in this body that we experience the pleasures of friendship, of love, of communicating.

We are strongly tied to our achievements; we cling to convictions we are fearful of losing, holding them tight in our fists. By behaving in this way, all we are doing is binding ourselves to the *body we have*, preventing the *body we are* from growing, from showing its true image.

It is our very bodies that, through their phases of evolution and their constant life-death-life dynamism, push us to leave the space we have won by going through a particular experience, in order to take control of another space further ahead, where we can go through another experience. This is the mechanism of life: *dying in order to live*. Staying still where they lie is proper to corpses – to those, that is, who no longer have anything to communicate, who have broken off all contact with others.

My body, then, cannot be simply *the body I have*: my life, in fact, is a continual *embodiment*. Through my senses, means that allow communication to take place, I allow the universe to come into me, I let myself be invaded by the world of others, of my friends and people I meet. In this way I join in the great discovery: I become aware, through the power of love, of passing from simple communication into deep communion. I experience the sensation of acquiring a new dimension, one that reaches beyond the space occupied by my physical body.

This *body I am* is no longer conditioned, constrained by the dimensions of time and space which affect the *body I have* and allow me to live the already exalting human experience. I perceive the power to welcome the infinite, and not alone, but myself being present in the infinite perceived by others.

This is the image of my body beginning to mature and to reveal those features that liken it to God. At the moment of the resurrection of the body these features will be perfected and I shall then truly be in a position to recognize *my body that I am*.

One day, in effect, *the body I have* will no longer be an obstacle and in opposition to *the body I am,* and so the two will tally. The life-death dialogue in which *the body I have dies* to give way to *the body I am* will take place for the last time: the caterpillar will become a butterfly. My *body of fleash* will give way to my *glorious body,* as the scriptures tell us, like unto the body of the risen Christ. Then indeed **communication will become communion.**

# PART TWO
# HANDS

Anatomical dictionaries give this simple definition:
"Extremities of the upper limbs of the human body."
Our two hands are the organs and the "symbol"
of human activity and its expression through gestures.
Together with speech they form one of the most
expressive modes of "human language."
Some Eastern peoples
hold their hands open towards them when they pray,
as though reading themselves.
Hands are "the book of life."
This is often a book many have not read:
so many of us don't know the language it is written in,
or have simply forgotten it.
The memory of when our hands first
raised a glass of water to our mouth . . .
scooped out a hollow in the sand . . .
tied a knot . . . drew a letter . . .
is too far back!
Perhaps the message conveyed to us then
seems to lack meaning,
and so the feelings each discovery,
each achievement aroused
have been overlaid by other sensations.
Perhaps we do not realize
that every action of ours
is really the product
of a fantastic effort of coordination
in which the whole person,
body-soul-spirit,
sets out its activity, its creativity.

# 5
# HUMAN HANDS

Hands can be warm, friendly, offered in fellowship.
But hands can be indifferent, conventional, cold, rough,
    hard,
pushing aside, putting down, refusing.
There are hands that open and hands that close,
clenched hands and hands held out,
opaque hands and hands you can see through.
A hand can calm, console, make safe,
or convey hatred, temper, despair.
A hand can say "goodbye" or "come here!"

*Gestures that manage to express the totality of being human, here*
*and now. Gestures that often need to be recognized and restored*
*to their deep significance, a significance often lost through habit*
*or overlaid by convention.*

The French sculptor **Auguste Rodin** (1840–1917) carved
two hands with the tips of the fingers joined and the
wrists slightly apart: he called this work "The Cathedral."

Two hands raised, one facing the other,
bend over till the tips of their fingers touch,
enclosing a little space that still holds
the promise of the entire heavens and their blessed
    immensity.
Every cathedral is a sacred space,

set apart from the noisy street of life,
withdrawn from the endless chatter that says nothing.
A cathedral collects and contains.
It welcomes prayers and great nostalgic dreams.
It dries tears and consoles those who weep.
It heals and soothes.
It softens and gathers light in a thousand colours.
It opens its doors and bids us enter in the name of a God
    who loves.
A cathedral lives on faithfulness.
God has promised it a blessing.
This blessing proclaims that life and all its days are
    "feast days."
A cathedral is a house that offers intimacy and invites us
    to take shelter in it.
By taking two simple hands and making a cathedral rise
    up,
Rodin has exactly recognized and artistically defined the
    essence of a hand.
**A hand is also the key to friendship, the key to holiness,**
**the key to . . . our home.**
*God holds out two hands to keep our soul in being, wide open.*
*God's hands are bridges thrown across to the world.*
*Our spirit and our heart walk over them.*
*They give our soul courage to try its utmost.*

Hands accept the wonders of the world.
They can chase after each other in a playful game.
They can whirl around our heads in joy, like windmills.
**In prayer they are like bowls held out for divine grace to**
    **be poured in.**
**Hands hold up a burning mirror to life:**
**they bewitch and surprise,**
**they bestow themselves,**
**arousing tenderness.**
**They make life smile.**

They are a safe stronghold with its doors barred,
and an inviting cathedral with its doors wide open.
Works of mercy, compassion, consolation
are wrought by hands.
Hands open doors.
Through hands, music is released,
smiles produced, and whirling dance.
Hands are instruments of work: they make roads,
    ditches, aircraft, churches, houses, clocks, toys.
They break down barriers and carve gargoyles.
They row and conquer.
They cook and feed.
They wash and iron.
They serve and calm.
They plant, cultivate and harvest.
*Hands are like God's messengers,*
*bestowing, welcoming and blessing.*
*In the sacraments they bring God's life home to us.*
*They link the poverty of the world to the riches of heaven.*
*And the blessing hand of God is there, holding out*
    *everlasting friendship.*

If human hands can also be predatory beasts
murdering and torturing, demolishing and wounding,
    tearing and laying waste . . .
. . . the times and the earth have better reason to await
    hands full of the blessings of goods and love:
capable of building, of encouraging,
of sowing seed that will germinate into an abundant and
    lasting harvest.
Hands that liberate and save.

**Leopold Segar Senghor** (1906- ), the Senegalese poet, gave
this wonderful description of hands:

**"A hand of light caresses my eyelids at night."**

Such a definition applies particularly to friends:

Hands make friendship blossom, and throw wide the
  door.
Hands make contact, one heart meeting another.
Hands welcome the other as a bodily sign and unite spirit
  to spirit.
A hand held out to another
  is a sign of readiness to welcome that other
  and to create an intense harmony.
A hand waving meets another
  and safely gives directions for the road ahead.
The hand that shakes another hand
  communicates a solid and happy union.
**The work of human hands cannot be reduced to**
  **the materiality of their actions:**
**in it, spirit and heart, soul and sensitivity, all meet.**
**Hands glide over hair, caressing,**
**they console and calm;**
**they beseech and implore;**
**they bring peace and wipe away tears.**
**They are robust in joy,**
**and impulsive in the play of love.**
**If, as they say,**
**creation was begun with**
**a hand,**
**then we can say that all friendship begins with**
**a hand.**
**And, finally, as Goethe said:**
**"Let this handshake say**
**what cannot be spoken."**

# 6
# HANDS IN THE LANGUAGE OF THE BIBLE

**Hands** in the Bible (Hebrew *yadaim,* Greek *kheires*) are the sign of human activity and a highly expressive mode of biblical language.

## (a) Washing One's Hands

This is not just a question of hygiene, but a **ritual gesture** designed to satisfy the requirements of legal purification, especially in relation to the priestly caste:

> *All those whom the sick man touches* **without washing his hands** *must wash their clothing and take a bath and will be unclean till evening* (Lev. 15:11).

> *Yahweh spoke to Moses and said, "You must also make a bronze basin on a stand, for washing. You must place it between the Tent of Meeting and the altar and put water in it. In this, Aaron and his sons must wash their hands and feet. When they are about to enter the Tent of Meeting they must wash in water lest they die, and when they have to approach the altar for their service, to burn the offering burned in honour of Yahweh, they must wash their hands and feet lest they die. This is a lasting rule for them, for Aaron and for his descendants from generation to generation* (Exod. 30:17–21).

We know the dispute related in the Gospels on this

subject, when Jesus' disciples were rebuked for sitting down to table with "unclean" hands:

> *One day the Pharisees with some teachers of the Law who had just come from Jerusalem gathered around Jesus. They noticed that some of his disciples were eating meat with unclean hands, that is, without washing them. Now the Pharisees, as well as the rest of the Jews, never eat without washing their hands for they observe the tradition received from their ancestors. Nor do they eat anything when they come from the market without first washing themselves. And there are many other traditions they observe, for example, the ritual washing of cups, pots and plates. So the Pharisees and the teachers of the Law asked him, "Why do your disciples not follow the tradition of the elders, but instead eat with unclean hands?"* (Mark 7:1–5).

See also Luke 11:37–8:

> *As Jesus was speaking, a Pharisee asked him to have a meal with him. So he went and sat at table. The Pharisee then wondered why Jesus did not first wash his hands before dinner.*

Washing one's hands becomes a "declaration of innocence":

> *Then all the elders of the city nearest to the man found dead shall wash their hands in the brook over the calf whose throat was cut. And they shall pronounce these words: "Our hands did not shed this blood, and our eyes did not see it. Forgive, O Yahweh, your people of Israel whom you rescued, and do not charge them with the shedding of innocent blood." So they shall be absolved from this blood, and you shall remove the guilt of innocent blood from your midst and do what is right in the eyes of Yahweh* (Deut. 21:6-9).

*I wash my hands free of guilt*
*and walk in procession round your altar,*
*singing in praise*
*and proclaiming your wondrous deeds* (Ps. 26:6-7).

*In vain have I kept my heart clean*
*and washed my hands in innocence.*
*All day long I have been stricken*
*and punished every morning* (Ps. 73:13–14).

Finally, remember Pilate's gesture at Jesus' trial:

*Pilate realized that he was getting nowhere and that instead*
*there could be a riot. He then asked for water and washed his*
*hands before the people, saying: "I am not responsible for his*
*blood. It is your doing"* (Matt. 27: 24).

### (b) Putting One's Hand over One's Mouth

This is the gesture made when one wants to remain silent, when "it's better not to say anything!":

*If you have been foolish enough to get angry*
*and afterwards regret it,*
*cover your mouth with your hand.*
*Since by churning the milk butter is produced,*
*by squeezing the nose blood flows,*
*and by stirring up anger arguments arise* (Prov. 30:32–3).

### (c) Covering One's Head with One's Hands

This is, above all, a gesture expressing **desperation and sorrow**, as the following passages show:

Tamar, raped by her brother Amnon, eldest son of King David, *put ashes on her head and tore the long robe she was wearing.* **Laying her hand on her head** *she went away crying aloud* (2 Sam. 13:19).

*You will be put to shame by Egypt as you were by Assyria.*
*You will also leave that place* **with your hands on your**
   **head,**
*for Yahweh has rejected those you trust,*
*and they will not help you!* (Jer. 2:36–7).

However, placing or laying hands on someone's head is also an expression of **blessing** or **well-wishing** or **showing the power of God**:

*Israel* **raised his right hand and placed it on Ephraim's head,** *although he was the younger, and placed his left hand on Manasseh's head even though he was the first-born. Then he blessed Joseph and said, "May the God in whose presence my fathers Abraham and Isaac walked, the God who has been my shepherd from my birth to this day, the Angel who has saved me from every evil, bless these boys* (Gen. 48:14–16a).

*People were bringing their little children to him that he might touch them, and the disciples scolded them for this (. . .) Then he took the children in his arms and* **laying his hands on them,** *blessed them* (Mark 10: 13, 16).

*He took the blind man by the hand and led him outside the village. When he had put spittle on his eyes* **and laid his hands upon him,** *he asked, "Can you see anything?"* (Mark 8:23).

*Seeing him, I fell at his feet like one dead, but he* **touched me with his right hand** *and said, "Do not be afraid. It is I, the First and the Last. I am the living one* (Rev. 1:17–18a).

*Do not neglect the spiritual gift conferred on you with*

*prophetic words when the elders* **laid their hands on you** (1 Tim. 4:14).

## (d) Shaking Hands

This is the gesture made to show agreement with the person one is speaking to. **It carries a particularly warm affective charge, as a sign of friendship**:

*Setting out from there, he met Jehonadab, son of Rechab, who came out to meet him. Jehu greeted him and said: "Would you be faithful to me as I am to you?" Jehonadab answered, "Yes." So Jehu said to him,* **"Give me your hand.** *He gave him his hand and Jehu took him up with him into his chariot, and said: "Come with me and see my zeal for Yahweh."* (2 Kings 10:15–16).

St Paul says in his Letter to the Galatians:

*They recognized that I have been entrusted to preach the Good News to the pagan nations, just as Peter has been entrusted to preach it to the Jews. In the same way that God made Peter the apostle of the Jews, he made me the apostle of the pagans. James, Peter and John acknowledged the graces God gave me. Those men who are regarded as the pillars of the Church* **stretched out their hand** *to me and Barnabas as a sign of fellowship; we would go to the pagans and they to the Jews. The only thing they asked us was to keep in mind the poverty of the brethren in Jerusalem; I have taken care to do this* (Gal. 2:7-10).

## (e) Taking Someone by the Hand

This is the gesture made by those who want to **lead someone** to a place, **guide him** along a road that may be unknown to him or difficult to follow.

This is what happened to Paul on the road to Damascus:

*Saul got up from the ground, but when he opened his eyes he could not see; **so they led him by the hand** and brought him into Damascus. He was blind for three days and took no food or drink* (Acts 8:8-9).
*"Yet the brightness of that light blinded me and I was **led by the hand** into Damascus by my companions"* (22:11).

Still in Acts, we read of Elymas the sorcerer, to whom Paul said:

*"Now the Lord's hand is upon you; you will become blind and for a time you will not see the light of day." At once a misty darkness came upon him and he groped about for someone **to lead him by the hand*** (13:11).

In the Psalms, this gesture becomes a **sign of faithfulness:**

*But my heart has been so embittered,*
*my spirit so distraught*
*that I failed to understand;*
*I was like a stupid beast in your presence.*
*Yet I shall always remain with you.*
***You take hold of my right hand,***
*you guide me with your counsel,*
*and in the end, you will take me to glory* (Ps. 73:21–4).

## (f) Clapping Hands

This is a gesture rich in various meanings, depending on the context in which it occurs.

It is a sign of **joy**:

***Clap your hands,*** *all you people;*
*acclaim God with shouts of joy and songs of praise* (Ps. 47:2).

It is a sign of **rage**:

*Balak's anger burned against Balaam; he **beat his hands together** and said: "I called you to curse my enemy and you have blessed him three times! So flee to your place now. I said I would greatly reward you but Yahweh has taken off your reward* (Num. 25:10–11).

It is a sign of **displeasure** or **distress**:

*This is what the Lord Yahweh said: **"Clap your hands,** stamp your feet and say: 'Well done!' when the people of Israel are falling by the sword, famine and plague because of their abominations"* (Ezek. 6:11).

*See, **I will clap my hands** at your dishonest profit, and the blood you have shed. Will your courage hold out, will your hands be steady, when I shall come against you? I, Yahweh, have spoken and I will act accordingly. I will scatter you among the nations, I will disperse you in other countries to rid you of your uncleanness. Then you will be dishonoured in the eyes of the nations and you will know that I am Yahweh* (22:13–16)

It is a sign of **pleasure in the misfortunes of others**:

*Passers-by shudder;*
***some clap their hands** at the sight;*
*others wag their heads at the fate*
*of the daughter of Jerusalem.*
*"Is this the city that was called*
*the loveliest, the joy of the world?"* (Lam. 2:15).

*Nothing can heal your wounds; your injury is fatal.*
***All clap their hands***
*when they hear about your fall.*

*For who has not suffered constantly*
*the plague of your cruelty?* (Nah. 3:19).

## (g) Praying with One's Hands

This is the gesture by which we communicate with God, and it involves our whole and entire being. Hands, with their expressive potentiality, here have an irreplaceable role, which will vary depending on the context of one's actual life-experience.

Hands can be lifted up in prayer:

*Lord, hear my voice and hasten to help me! Listen to my plea when I call to you.*
*Let my prayer rise to you like incense, and **my hands be lifted up as in an evening sacrifice*** (Ps. 141:1–2).

Hands can be raised to heaven to swear an oath calling on God as witness. This is what Abraham does in reply to the King of Sodom:

*The King of Sodom said to Abraham, "Give me the people and keep the goods for yourself." Abraham said to the King of Sodom, "**I raise my hand** to Yahweh God Most High, creator of heaven and earth, to swear that not one thread or thong of a sandal, or anything that is yours, would I take"* (Gen. 14:21–3).

A hand can be raised to one's mouth as a sign of adoration (reminding one of the popular etymology of *adorare = ad os = to the mouth*):

*If I have put my trust in gold*
*or have sought my security from it,*
*if I have gloated over my wealth,*

*my fortune and my accomplishments,*
*if I have regarded the sun in its radiance*
*or the moon in its splendour,*
*and having been enticed offered them*
**a kiss of my hand** *in homage,*
*then these also would be sins to judge*
*for I would have been unfaithful to God* (Job 31:24–8).

Stretching out one's hand symbolizes power with its two components of strength and ability, both in the physical and spiritual fields. The recurrent expression "to give into the hands of," means "to make subject to":

*Yahweh said to Moses, "Why do you cry to me? Tell the people of Israel to go forward. You will raise your staff and* **stretch your hand** *over the sea" (. . .) Moses stretched his hand over the sea and Yahweh made a strong east wind blow all night and dry up the sea. The waters divided and the sons of Israel went on dry ground through the middle of the sea (. . .) The Egyptians followed them (. . .) Then Yahweh said to Moses, "Stretch you hand over the sea and let the waters come back over the Egyptians, over their chariots and horsemen." Moses* **stretched out his hand** *over the sea. At daybreak the sea returned to its place. As the Egyptians tried to flee, Yahweh swept them into the middle of the sea. (The Israelites) understood what wonders Yahweh had done for them against Egypt, and the people feared Yahweh. They believed in Yahweh and in Moses, his servant* (Exod. 14:15–31).

*"Be strong and stand firm; be fearless, be confident when you face the King of Assyria and the whole army he brings with him, since he that is with us is stronger than he that is with him. He has* **only an arm of flesh,** *but we have Yahweh our God to help us and fight our battles." The people were encouraged by the words of Hezekiah king of Judah* (2 Chron. 32:7-8).

49

### (h) The Hands of God

The anthropological symbol is also applied to the action of God. This is why the expression "hand of God" or "arm of God" is found so often in the Bible.

After the crossing of the Reed Sea, Moses sings a song of praise to Yahweh:

> *Thy right hand, O Lord, is majestic in strength:*
> *Thy right hand, O Lord, shattered the enemy*
> *In the fullness of thy triumph,*
> *Thou didst cast the rebels down* (Exod. 15:6-7).

Deuteronomy generally uses the expression "outstretched arm," which goes with the "firm hand" of God:

> *Never has there been a God who went out to look for a people and take them out from among the other people by the strength of trials and signs, by wonders and by war, **with a firm hand and an outstretched arm**. Never has there been any deed as tremendous as those done for you by Yahweh in Egypt, which you saw with your own eyes* (4:34).

> *Remember that you were once enslaved in the land of Egypt from where Yahweh, your God, brought you out **with his powerful hand and outstretched arm*** (5:15).

> *Perhaps you will say in your heart, "These nations are more numerous than I am, how then am I going to drive them away?" Do not be afraid, remember what Yahweh, your God, has done with Pharaoh and with the Egyptians, those terrible plagues which you saw with your eyes and the marvels and signs, **the strong hand and outstretched arm** with which Yahweh, your God, has freed you* (7:17–19).

> *The Egyptians maltreated us, oppressed us and subjected us to*

50

*harsh slavery. So we called to Yahweh, the God of our fathers, and Yahweh listened to us. He saw our humiliation, our hard labour and the oppression to which we were subjected. He brought us out of Egypt **with a firm hand**, manifesting his power with signs and awesome wonders. And he brought us here to give us this land flowing with milk and honey (26:6-9).*

The hand of the Lord is seen, then, in Moses; it also appears in Elijah and Elisha (1 and 2 Kings), in Isaiah and Ezekiel, and in the figure of the suffering Servant:

*Thus says God, Yahweh (. . .)*
*I, Yahweh, have called you for the sake of justice;*
***I will hold your hand** to make you firm;*
*I will make you a covenant to the people*
*and as a light to the nations,*
*to open eyes that do not see,*
*to free captives from prison,*
*to bring out to light those who sit in the darkness*
*(Isa. 42:6-7).*

*Listen to me, O islands,*
*pay attention, peoples from distant lands.*
*Yahweh called me from my mother's womb;*
*he pronounced my name before I was born.*
*He made my mouth like a sharpened sword.*
***He hid me in the shadow of his hand.***
*He made me into a polished arrow*
*set apart in his quiver (49:1-2).*

*Who could believe what we have heard,*
*And to whom has the **strong arm** of Yahweh been revealed?*
*Like a root out of dry ground,*
*like a sapling he grew up before us,*
*with nothing attractive in his appearance,*
*no beauty, no majesty (53:1-2).*

In the **New Testament**, too, the theme of **the hand of the Lord** is taken up again:

On the occasion of the birth of John the Baptist, we read that:

> *A holy fear came on all in the neighbourhood, and throughout the Hills of Judah the people talked about these events. As they heard this, they pondered it in their minds and wondered, "What will this child be?" For they understood that **the hand of the Lord** was with him* (Luke 1:55–6).

At the end of the great debates between Jesus and the Jews, at the time of the feast of Dedication in Jerusalem, Jesus declares:

> *My sheep hear my voice and I know them, they follow me and I give them eternal life. They shall never perish and no one will ever steal them from me. What the Father has given me is stronger than everything and no one can snatch it **from the Father's hand**. I and the Father are one* (John 10:27–30).

Finally, let us recall Jesus' last words on the cross, in which he entrusts himself to the Father, using verse 6 of Psalm 31:

*Then Jesus gave a loud cry, "Father, I commend my spirit into your hands." And after he said that, he gave up his spirit* (Luke 23:46).

The **"power"** of God's arm appears in Mary's *Magnificat*:

*He has shown the **power of his arm**,*
*He has routed the proud of heart* (Luke 1:51).

Another variant is the **"finger of God"**:

> *But suppose I am driving out demons **by the finger of God**;*
> *would not this mean that the kingdom has come among you?*
> *(Luke 11:20, recalling Exod. 8:15: The magicians said to*
> *Pharaoh, "This is **the finger of God**"; but Pharaoh was*
> *unmoved and did not listen, as Yahweh had foretold.)*

## (i) The Right Hand of God

The people of the Bible *oriented* (the verb itself says it)
themselves, turned to the East, to the rising sun. When
they did this, the South came to be "on their right hand,"
which then came to be regarded as the propitious side, as
it was filled with the light of the sun; the North, then,
became "the left hand," and was unfavourable because it
pointed to sunset and the darkness of night. This is where
the phrase "sit on my right hand," meaning giving a place
of honour, takes its full meaning from.

> *So Bathsheba went to King Solomon to speak to him on behalf*
> *of Adonijah. The king met her and bowed to her. Then he sat*
> *on his throne and had a seat brought for the king's mother,*
> ***who sat on his right**. She said, "I have one small request to*
> *make of you. Do not refuse me." And the king answered her,*
> *"Make your request, my mother, for I will not refuse you."*
> *(1 Kings 2:19–20).*

The same theme is taken up again in Psalm 45:10:

> *Among your ladies of honour*
> *are daughters of kings;*
> ***at your right hand,** in gold of Ophir,*
> *stands the queen.*

The Psalmist sings with confidence:

> *I bless the Lord who counsels me;*
> *even at night, my inmost self instructs me.*
> *I keep the Lord always before me;*
> *for with him **at my right hand** – never*
> *will I be shaken or troubled.*
> *My heart, therefore, exults, my soul rejoices;*
> *my body, too, will rest assured* (16:7-9).

> *The Lord says to my Lord,*
> *"Sit at my right hand*
> *till I make your foes your footstool."* (110:1).

This is a messianic Psalm particularly dear to the New Testament, in which it is cited or referred to a good twenty-five times. This is why it is said that Jesus is "seated at the right hand of God," who has made him "Lord and Christ."

> *This Messiah is Jesus and we are all witnesses that God raised*
> *him to life. He has been exalted **at God's right side** and the*
> *Father has entrusted the Holy Spirit to him; this Spirit he has*
> *just poured upon us as you now see and hear.*
> *David did not ascend into heaven, but he himself said:*
> *"The Lord said to my Lord:*
> *sit **at my right side***
> *until I make your enemies a stool for your feet."*
> *Let Israel then know that God has made Lord and Christ this*
> *Jesus whom you crucified* (Acts 2:32–6).

So Jesus exalted at the "**right hand**" of God, has been given the Holy Spirit which he has then given to his disciples.

See Acts 2:33 just cited, and:

*The God of our ancestors raised Jesus whom you killed by hanging him on a wooden post. God set him **at his right hand** as Leader and Saviour, to grant repentance and forgiveness of sins to Israel. We are witnesses to all these things, as well as the Holy Spirit whom God has given to those who obey him* (Acts 5:30–2).

The exaltation of the just, at the final judgment, will take place in glory **"at the right hand of the Son of man"**:

*When the Son of man comes in his glory with all his angels, he will sit on the throne of Glory. All the nations will be brought before him, and as a shepherd separates the sheep from the goats, so will he do with them, placing the sheep **on his right** and the goats on his left.*

*The King will say **to those on his right:** "Come, blessed of my Father! Take possession of the kingdom prepared for you from the beginning of the world"* (Matt. 25:31–4).

# 7
# THE LANGUAGE OF OUR HANDS

If this work were to end here, we should have achieved no more than a purely intellectual exercise, one that could easily be sterile, an end in itself. The course we are undertaking together, however, means that we now need to *verify* if and how far we can relate or reconcile our outlook with that of the people of the Bible in their dialogue with God.

This alone will enable us to discover whether the codes of the symbolic language of hands, brought out in the Bible, are *meaningful* for us in our time.

Here we are, then, specifically invited to discover, describe and interiorize the great expressive and creative potential of *our hands*, distinguishing their symbolic language when they move or when they are still; when they close or open; as we push them away or bring them forward; as they put something together or take it apart; when and how they react to softness, smoothness, hardness, roughness; when they arouse pleasure or provoke annoyance; when they bless or curse . . . .

**Hands speak to each of us to the degree that we know how to recognize their means of expression.** They therefore need to be *observed* for a space of time; we need to *contemplate* their movements, even the simplest and most spontaneous ones; we need to *discern* the smallest sensations they are able and wish to communicate to us.

To help us learn to do these things, there follows a

series of **practical exercises** to go through, starting with recognizing the expressive capacity of our hands, going on to reading their symbolic language, and ending by using this language in our relationship with God, in prayer.

## PRACTICAL EXERCISES

### A. Cognition and Re-cognition of Our Hands

*Objectives*
(a) To observe our own hands in all their separateness and togetherness, comparing the right with the left, in order to acquire the experience necessary to re-cognize them as ours among all other hands.
(b) To pick out the similarities between our two hands and also the particularities that distinguish them as right hand and left hand.

*Aim*
We are trying to experience contemplation, in a way we perhaps seldom do. Then we relate our discoveries to the sensations that emerge in relation to the particular experience of the person we are here and now. Then we let our feelings for that person, whether of acceptance or rejection, flow out.

*Starting point*
First, we need to carry out an exercise in relaxation so as to create the proper conditions for observation and contemplation. This means:

* Sitting, perhaps on a rug on the floor;
* Controlling our breathing and heartbeat;
* Cultivating an inner calm.

EXERCISE 1
Look carefully at your hands; first one and then the other,

in different positions: relaxed, tensed, clenched in a fist, with the fingers splayed; move your fingers one by one, slowly at first, then faster and faster, continuously or stopping and starting. Watch each action carefully. Then touch as you watch: the right hand touching each part of the left – joints, muscles, bones – and vice-versa; notice the difference between fingers, how they can move – forwards, backwards, right, left, in a circle, up and down –; feel the discomfort or pain caused by moving them too sharply or keeping them constrained; observe: the particular colour they take on in each position, the texture of the skin, marks of scars, veins, hairs, nails, callouses . . . . Notice all the differences between one hand and the other, and between the backs and the palms.

EXERCISE 2
(If these exercises are being carried out in a group.)
Once you each know your own hands well enough, invite the participants to form pairs. Seated one in front of the other, try to get to know the other person's hands so as to establish the differences from and similarities to your own.

Once you have got to know the other's hands, clasp both his/her hands in both of your own and stay like this for a time, looking at each other and taking stock of the feelings and emotions aroused. If possible, pay particular attention to your breathing and the pace of your heartbeat: this will enable you to become aware of how a single part of the body can involve the whole body in its activity, by acting to change the rate of your breathing and heartbeat.

*Observations*
These exercises should be carried out slowly, without haste and, if necessary, repeated several times: the important thing is for each phase to sink well in, because this is the only way for a new understanding to come about.

We need to bear in mind that the purpose of these exercises is not to get to know "new" parts of our body, or to be able to name the various bits, but rather to allow an experience to emerge, one linked to all segments or a particular movement of our hands and brought about by feelings of rejection or acceptance, of sorrow or joy.

*Feedback*

We need to establish:

* that we have really come to re-cognize the characteristics that typify our hands, so as to distinguish them from all others;

* that we are clear about the similarities and differences between our right hand and our left. Once we have done this, we can try to put our discoveries into words, or communicate them through mime, or, better still, by acting them. In doing so, we should above all distinguish the details or experiences of rejection and acceptance and learn to understand their symbolic meaning: what they are really trying to tell us.

## B. The "Mark" of Our Hands

*Objectives*

(a) To notice and describe the external characteristics of our hands as they express what we do = **backs**.

(b) To recognize that all our activity or relations with things and with other people leave a mark, an "imprint" that denotes our individuality = **palms**.

*Aim*

To realize that every intervention, every communicative relationship, of ours with nature or with other people, leaves a *mark*. *It is absolutely impossible for us to pass "unnoticed"* through the history in which we are living: all our actions are stamped with our personal mark, unique to us.

*Starting Point*

Provide yourself with several sheets of white (typing or drawing) paper, a pencil, some coloured crayons, poster paints in the basic colours (green, blue, yellow, red) and a fine paint brush.

Prepare yourself mentally to listen hard to your own body and to be serenely open to the study of your own hands.

EXERCISE 1

*Draw your own hands*

Place one hand on a sheet of white paper.

Draw round it with the pencil.

Take the hand away and fill in the details (of the back of your hand, of course!) with the pencil, noting all the details you manage to observe: each line, all the shadings, the pattern of veins . . . .

Finally, colour the drawing with the crayons.

Then carry out the same operation with the other hand.

All these operations will, of course, have to be done with the "other" hand, that is, the one you are not actually using as a model to draw from.

*Observations*

\* Drawing and describing our hands will bring out our own capacity for observation: observe how some details seem more important than others. Why? What experiences do they suggest? What feelings emerge or are brought out?

\* In this way we are "brought up against" the limits to our powers of observation and our subjectivity and the way we tend to select our perceptions of how we are and how we relate to things and other people.

\* This exercise also helps us to understand the difficulty we find in communicating to others what "concerns" us, what is "ours": communication through words or gestures is always a reduction of the reality, or an attempt to adapt it to the framework of a language.

In daily life, this forms the stimulus for arousing:

– first, a sense of humility, in that we know ourselves to be limited and incomplete;

– second, an openness to others, in that we seek to be completed.

\* The instruction to use the "other" hand, the one that is not the object of our observation, is designed to make us understand the different working ability of the left and right sides of our body, or a part of them.

## EXERCISE 2
### *The imprint of my hands*
Still using a sheet of white paper, and now the poster paints, press your hands down on to the paper, after coating them in a colour of your choice.

*Observations*

The imprint will be that of the palm of your hands. But it won't be a perfect impression. This is characteristic of any sort of direct printing process: it is an imperfect reproduction of a reality, and furthermore, a mirror-image of the original, an element that makes it harder to read.

\* This characteristic is used here to signify the particular expressive quality of our actions. In effect, in all our dealings with things and other people, we leave our "special mark," an aspect, a plain trace of our own reality – of our experience, that is, not of the whole of ourselves.
\* The imprint is not the person, though it may be a sign by which the person can be recognized. It is a symbol of the person's whole being and experience: a unique, individual, unrepeatable stamp.

*Feedback*
\* Learn how to distinguish some characteristic signs of the imprint left by your hands.

* Allowing memory of experiences to surface, pick out a particular moment in which each one of your hands has been in the forefront, either in a positive or a negative role, leaving a characteristic mark.

## C. Working Hands

### (i) My Hands

*Objective*

To understand the specific activity of our hands in our overall activity as a person.

*Aim*

This exercise provides a time for contemplation of and reflection on the activity proper to our hands in the overall complex of a person's experience, both in the present moment and at times in past life.

What movements have been required of our hands to carry out those activities we have been engaged in during the course of our day or of a period in our life?

*Starting Point*

Sit down, perhaps on the ground, with your hands free to move in any direction.

Find a position in which you are balanced and relaxed. Visualize your surroundings, including the other people around you (if you are doing this exercise in a group).

Bring yourself to a state of inner calm.

EXERCISE

Taking time, contemplate your own hands, moving them about and touching one with the other.

Review in your memory the actions you have carried out during the day, or at a particular time of your life, picking out the actual way your hands functioned in some of the actions under review: how they moved, what they touched, what sensations or perceptions they communicated, etc.

The various experiences you recall will cover a wide range of activity and of expressive capability, and this is characteristic of our hands.

*Observations*
* This should be a contemplation carried out very slowly, with no time limit set.
* At any hint of tiredness or distraction, stop for a few moments, or change position, or move to a different spot.
* Avoid any reasoned attempt to structure your contemplation conceptually. Rather, let your feelings arise spontaneously.

*Feedback*
* Ask yourself: "If I had not had my hands, how would I have acted in this or that situation?"
* Go over in detail and describe the movements carried out by your hands in two particular actions during the day or during a period of your life, and let sensations of them emerge: Have I understood why I used my right hand instead of my left? Why the palm rather than the back? Why the thumb and index finger, and not the thumb and little finger?

### (ii) Other People's Hands

*Objectives*
(a) To understand the expressive language of other people's hands while they perform actions typical of their craft or occupation.
(b) To learn to understand this language by observing the results of their actions or looking at a pictorial representation of them (a photo or drawing).

*Aim*
* Having come to know and understand the expressive

capabilities of our own hands and the important part they play in carrying out what we ask of them,
* it now becomes important to take stock of the works performed by the hands of other people, works that enable them to live their lives, such as: living in a house, crossing a street, eating bread, drinking water, dressing, reading, drawing . . . ,
* or what they might do to condition and limit them: pulling things down, making people suffer, destroying the ecological balance, killing . . . .

*Starting Point*
Seated or standing in a part of the room you choose, take stock of the space you effectively occupy at the moment. Guide yourself to a state of inner calm.

EXERCISE 1
* Visualize your surroundings: walls, cupboards, books, chairs, tables, lamps . . . .
* Let one of these objects enter into harmony with you, with your experience.
* Imagine the work that has gone into bringing it into being, and being here, concentrating above all on the actions carried out by hands in the process of bringing it into being and in the fact of its being here now.
* In your memory, go over all the movements involved in these actions, letting the various emotions associated with them flow out.

EXERCISE 2 ·
* Spread out on the floor photographs chosen to emphasize the activities people perform with their hands and the results of these activities.
* Look at all these photographs, trying to grasp the message they are seeking to convey to you, and to enter into dialogue with them. This is a matter of taking a stroll down the streets of a "symbolic" world that can stimulate

the *evocation* of an experience and come into harmony with us, here and now.

* Having taken this stroll, and having selected from it the mesage most appropriate to our present, pick up the photograph that corresponds most closely to it, choose a place, sit down and compose yourself to contemplate all it tells you and the harmonious chords it is capable of striking in you. Give free rein to the emotions it produces.

*Observations*

In either the first or the second exercise, it may happen that the object or the photograph chosen can communicate aspects of the message that we failed to notice at first: a detail that, unforeseen, carries a strong evocative charge.

In such a case, it is advisable to retain this new impulse, since its appearance is less subject to the defences usually put up by reason, and it is therefore truer, because unforeseen, and has greater emotive depth: a message has been conveyed to me independently of my choice . . . and all I am asked to do is accept it.

*Feedback*

Going over the exercise in our minds should show how far we have understood, as being like our own, the linguistic-expressive code used by others. Are we capable of distinguishing a constructive from a destructive activity, both in the movements of hands and in their results?

### D. Hands in the Relationship between Experience and Expression

*Objectives*

(a) To examine the behaviour of hands and their capacity to communicate and arouse feelings:
– in an encounter with an "object";
– in an encounter with another person.

(b) To observe and note the relationship between a person's overall experience and the expressive-symbolic gestures of their hands alone as they try to communicate and sum up this experience.

*Observations*
* The first thing we need to do in pursuing these objectives is to be ready to overcome the routine and feelings of flatness imposed on us by our daily lives. The repetitiveness of actions, the levelling out of feelings and the boredom of meetings threaten to stifle all efforts at creativity, novelty, pleasure in self-expression and communicating.
* On the other hand, our whole expressive potentiality is necessarily bound up in the day-to-day, unless our behaviour is a cold and rational theatrical performance in which we refuse to become truly involved.
* It will, probably, be a matter of accepting the daily routine, while trying to subject it to a "re-discovery" through an understanding of our own capacities for recognizing our experience and discovering ways in which to express it.

EXERCISE 1
*The Expressive Gestures of Hands in an*
*Encounter with an "Object"*
* This is rather a "description" of an experience than a proposal for something to do. This means that it is a subjective exercise, and can be be more than a simple indication of how to stimulate reflection on how we observe our own experience and that of others.
* We call an "object" anything that can be used, made instrumental, manipulated freely, without being able to oppose a resistance of the same intensity as our purpose with it.

We can also take the same attitudes to persons as we take to a "thing," be it animal or inanimate. But here we are keeping the two approaches quite separate, simply because the second deals with the expression of a personal human reality, that of a "subject."

* So, taking the classic format of an encounter, we can direct our observations to certain stages of this and concentrate our attention on the gestures made by our hands, taking these as capable of expressing the feelings, emotions and choices of our whole body, of our whole person, that is.

* *Let us follow these stages with the aid of of four photographic images:*

(1) The "object" in question is a a young bird, a baby Kingfisher: it has perhaps left its nest too early, before it can fly properly, and has fallen on to the sand on a river bank. It hasn't enough strength to fly away on its own.

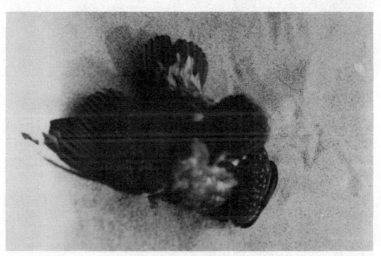

A girl comes running along the bank, and notices it. It inspires her with feelings of pity: "Poor little thing . . . how small it is! It's all alone . . . perhaps it's wounded . . . but it's so pretty! Look at its long, black beak, and all the colours of its feathers! What a bright blue!"

(2) But it is not just the bird's beak and feathers that appeal to the girl's feelings: she is seeing a situation much like her own. She too is a little being; she too is "alone" in her process of growing up and facing the problems of life; even if there are lots of people around her, she feels the need of someone to take her part, while at the same time she feels a need to be left in peace to try to do things through her own efforts . . . .

Then what happens is this: the girl's hands make her body bend down; she stretches her arms out towards the bird, as though to meet it. Her hands open, and then close round the little body, in a gesture of protection, as though wanting and trying to re-create a warm and secure nest for it.

(3) The pleasure aroused by this encounter brings a desire to continue the contact, to set up a relationship.

But this desire is shown in a gesture and attitude of

*possession*, of "privatization," almost of seizure, of absorption of the "other's" viewpoint into one's own. The nest, then, becomes no longer a warm and secure refuge, but more like an enclosure, a cage, an attempt to prevent the bird from breaking off the "dialogue" by flying away.

(4) In the end, however, the girl too feels a desire for freedom; she feels, that is, the need to offer the little bird what is so important to her: to be, and to be able to express oneself as, *free*.

Her hands open, and so become a springboard for a gift of openness and impetus toward the possibility of going out to meet "the world."

EXERCISE 2
*The Expressive Gestures of Hands in the
Encounter with Another Person*
\* Since we are here dealing with two "subjects," so two beings capable of actively expressing their own feelings, their own emotions, dialogue and rejection of dialogue, the ways in which an encounter can take place will be that much more varied and complicated.

While maintaining their own characteristics, the two human freedoms should each be well aware of the attitudes of the other, and the particular way in which they both display their outlook, if only through similar gestures, capable of speaking in the same code of symbolic language.

\* We need, naturally, to pay attention to the symbolic expressions of our hands, because we are investing them with the capacity to communicate the emotive charge of the whole human person.

\* The situation described here is presented by way of example rather than as a model, in that the description is of a specific situation seen in relation to a particular state of mind. Obviously, in reality, things could work out quite differently.

\* So, what we need to do now is to follow through this encounter, visualizing it, and thereby discovering the emotive reactions that follow from it, concentrating our attention on the expressive language of hands.

(1) **Two people meet:** they approach each other and display a mutual willingness to establish and deepen a dialogue. To this, they both bring their consciousness of their own individuality, their own outlook.

*Let us concentrate on what they do with their hands:* these express a welcoming attitude; they are actively open to dialogue and conscious of being able to express a personality, while also being ready and willing to defend this from any threat of attack, and, at the same time, willing to "risk" the unforeseen consequences of a relationship with the other person. In the case illustrated in the photos, the difference between the two people is brought out by their different skin colours.

(2) **Now, contact has been made and established**: the difference between the two people is shown here by the relative position of their hands (which could, of course, have been the other way round):

– one hand, the black one, is in the shape of a *cup*, showing capacity to receive;
– the other is like water being poured out, like a *gift* capable of fulfilling, of satisfying.

The action takes place calmly: there is a complete absence of any attempt to impose one on the other. At this point different reactions in response to the encounter can well be noted (feedback).

(3) **Having made contact, the two hands close over each other in the typical gesture of meeting.** By mutually placing a part – and such an expressive part – of their own bodies in contact with one another, the two people wish to show (or should do, at least!) their own availability, their desire not to close themselves off from at least a superficial understanding, which might, of course, be the sign of the beginning of a deeper collaboration.

In our culture, shaking another person's hand is seen as a cordial gesture, one invoking friendship, assent and agreement. But of course the gesture, to be read accurately, needs to be seen in relation to other bodily movements that accompany it and back it up. So while shaking hands, we may:

– slap the other person on the back with our other hand;
– slightly bend our head forward as a sign of deference;
– or keep our body ramrod straight on its feet . . . .

(4) **A further response or next step** may be signified by an affective understanding, expressing willingness to "travel a stretch of the road" together, in an emotional sharing of respective points of view, but at the same time respecting one another's individuality, while doing so in tenderness and with pleasure. This is the usual gesture of a boy and girl wishing to communicate and share affection and tenderness between one another.

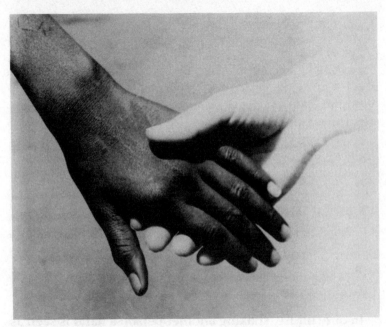

(5) **Time passes, the encounter matures** and the dialogue deepens: the outlooks of the two subjects can come so close that they merge into one and form a unity. Neither of the two personalities is impoverished by this; rather, the new experience produces "new things": a marvellous creativity emerges and and from it something completely original and new is born, something that can be expressed in a unique fashion through their relationship with things and with other people.

Their hands intertwine: they become the symbol of being a couple – in the widest sense (so not necessarily a married couple!).

These images and the interpretations of them we have given, of course provide only some aspects of a possible description of such an encounter.

If our hands, then, as we have said, are the image of the whole person by reason of their expressive capabilities, they take on, as they communicate, the specific characteristics of each individual, in that they reveal her/his life experience.

In this context, and before going on to consider the expressive relationship *"person-hands"*, it might be interesting to look at these two pictures which illustrate by contrast the different outcomes of an encounter: the reality of the two people and the actual situations that make up their experience, in fact determine the ways in which they will act in an encounter.

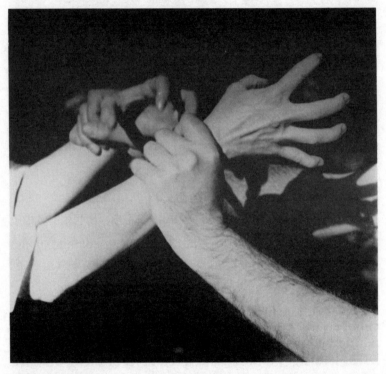

**(a) Aggressivity and Defence**
– the attacker's hands look like the talons of a bird of prey ready to grab its victim: they express nervous tension above all, shown by veins and tendons standing out and the rigidity of the fingers.
– the defender's hands close like a vice in order to neutralize the efforts of the attacker.

**(b) Solidarity and Help**
– the strong, generous helper is in a higher position, and
the fingers of his hands firmly grasp the wrists of – the
weaker partner in need of help, who, being lower down,
tries to close his fingers round the forearms of his helper,
. . . the two together making something like a reef knot in
a rope.

Finally, we now need to see whether, for each of us as
well, these gestures can be read by using an interpretative-
symbolic code similar to the one described above.

**EXERCISE 3**
*The Expressive Relationship between:*
*a Person's Experience-based Attitude and*
*the Language of Hands*

Let us now try to proceed to the discovery of certain expressive techniques proper to our hands.

Here we shall limit ourselves to some illustrative examples, from which each of us can make personal deductions useful for reading expressive symbols. These examples can also be used as:
– useful material for checking;
– stimuli for exploring new expressive forms;
– tools for critical analysis of the validity of this way of relating our experience to the symbolic-expressive capacity of just one part of our bodies, in this case, our hands.

## (1) A Family: father-mother-child
*The position we take up with our bodies usually indicates the intensity of our relationship with other people.* In this case, the child is clearly the centre of its parents' attention.

– Effectively, in the figurative photograph opposite, this centrality is shown by **the direction they are looking in.**
– In the symbolic photograph below, the same effect is produced **by the way the two adult hands are held open to receive the child's hand.**

In both pictures, communication comes about both through physical contact and by means of symbolic expression.

Besides this, the calm and relaxed atmosphere favours an attitude of reciprocal communication within the family, and, furthermore, a communication not closed in on itself, but **open to the outside world.** This openness is both shown and signified by the child

78

– **looking straight at the camera, and**
– **having the palm of its open hand facing upwards,** as if to show willingness to dialogue and capacity for acceptance being transmitted from one person to another.

**(2) Protection and security: an adult and two children in a situation of danger and instability**

This is an experience that produces pleasure but, at the same time, places the protagonists in a risk situation.

– We are in the mountains, sitting on a ledge; below us, the void; in front of us, a marvellous view invites our contemplation. **The adult is pledged to guarantee safety, so that the view can be contemplated with serenity.**

– The symbolic photograph expresses the same situation: **the adult's hand comes down from above; it holds the child's hand firmly, strongly.** The fingers of the child's hand are folded into the grip of the powerful adult hand, but its arm denotes calm and security stemming from the protection it is receiving.

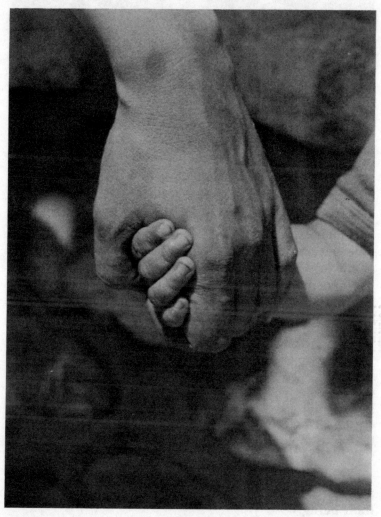

### (3) Quest for security and affection: a father-daughter relationship

– In the figurative photograph, **the relationship** is shown by playing on a beach. The position of the two bodies indicates *intense communicativeness and pleasure in being quietly together, without worries.*

When the smallest and weakest look for security and affection, they do so quite naturally, and are happy to find anyone who can provide them.

– In the symbolic photo, the "vice" grip of the child on the adult *is not a sign of constraint or conditioning,* but allows both to show what they are, and, at the same time, to maintain a dialogal independence to the degree required to communicate. The girl's body is small and cannot enfold her father's; she nevertheless manages to enfold the big thumb she clings on to.

**Adults, big people, tend to enfold what they protect.**

**Children, weak people, don't. They don't impose in asking for help; they just communicate the limitations of their being!**

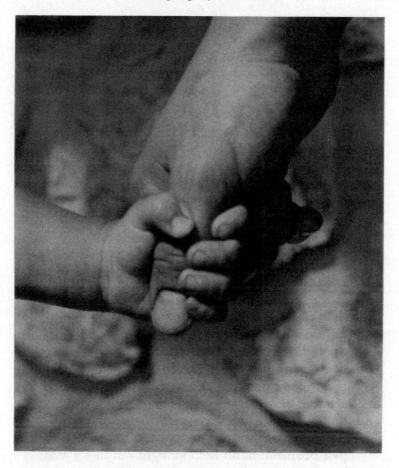

Many other examples could be given to describe the relationship between people's life-situation and the symbolic language of their hands. The few given, however, should be enough to make the concept clear.

*It is now up to each of you to discover this symbolic language in your own situation and experience, to take charge of it and make use of it in the wonderful dynamism of communication.*

# 8
# THE SYMBOLIC LANGUAGE OF OUR HANDS

**First Considerations**

* But is it really true that hands have a linguistic code of their own? Yes, provided that their gestures express a message and that this message is communicated with respect for linguistic conventions. Provided that, that is, **the subject is saying something to someone.**

* Let us take just the three basic positions hands adopt spontaneously, either to accompany verbal communication, or to take its place, in so far as they are capable, on their own, of expressing the outlook of the whole person. In effect, these are gestures made in relation to our state of mind, either reinforcing it or replacing it:

    – **rest position**: hand relaxed, in the shape of a *cup*;
    – **open position**: hand held straight out like a *road*;
    – **closed position**: hand closed into a fist like a *stone*.

These three positions are typical expressions of **symbolic body language**.

* By "the language of our hands" we mean:
    – non-verbal, gestural language, or
    – non-vocal language.

Some gestures are, in fact, capable of expressing the meaning of a word exactly and so can take its place:

"Silence!" – index finger held against the lips, as though to keep the mouth shut; "O.K.!" or "Go ahead!" – a quick forward flick of the hand, stopping abruptly with the hand closed and the index finger held up . . . .

* *"Taking the place of . . . going beyond the material aspect of gesture"*: it is just this that makes such a language symbolic.

* Consequently: *the integrity and efficacy of the message are directly proportionate to its capacity to convey this symbolic language.*

A difficulty can, however, arise from the interlocutor's incapacity to decipher the codes of this language: in such cases the communication is sterile. *In order to communicate, it is not enough to know the complex of linguistic codes. It is, rather, vital to use a language the hearer can understand.*

* The effectiveness of a message will depend, either
  – on *understanding* of the symbolic language, or
  – on our capacity to *"use"* it properly.

Developing this effectiveness will be the *objective* in the exercises that follow.

* It is important to note that the three positions given above, being immediately dependent on the efforts of muscles and tendons, have been chosen as capable of expressing particular feelings shared by people of all ages and all cultures.

Consequently, the messages they convey should be **universally understandable** in that they make up the **non-verbal language proper to the human body** and express, genuinely and adequately, the situation of the **being** of each person.

## Hands

### Preparatory Exercise

*Objectives*
(a) To observe our hands in movement and at rest in order to remind ourselves of their linguistic code and their expressive potential.
(b) To remind ourselves, once again, of their numerous activities in the context of our overall experience.

*Aim*
\* To recall, in particular, the exercises given in the previous section, in which we tried to approach the nature and working capabilities of our hands as agents of communication, with a view to
\* bringing out the three main positions: rest, open, closed, which concern us in what follows in respect of their symbolic language.

*Starting Position*
Sit on your heels, or with your legs crossed, head and chest erect so as to avoid strain on your muscles or inner organs; your arms hang by your sides and your hands rest on the floor, palms up.

### EXERCISE

\* Slowly raise your hands, bending your elbows, and rest your hands on your thighs, just above your knees, palms facing up.
\* Look at them carefully: they are still, relaxed. Your breathing is calm and regular, your body not subject to any strain.
\* Little by little your hands begin to move, as though wakening from sleep.
\* Your fingers start a little dance, slow at first and then quicker, more excited . . . then slowing down again and eventually going back to the rest position they started

86

from, almost as though trying to sink back into the sleep from which they had been awakened.

* Realize that these are your hands: how many things we do with our hands! From the moment we wake up to the time we go to sleep, they are in continuous movement, expressing all that we do.

* They do what we ask them to. And yet they often send messages which we in vain try to hold back, not to understand or communicate. And then they say so many things which we should never be capable of expressing in words.

*Observations*

– We could really say that our hands "**speak**" when our mouths don't. Their words cannot be heard with ears: we have to *observe* them carefully, learn their language, in order to understand the message they contain.

– Perhaps they have a truer means of "**saying**" than the verbal one, being less subject to the control of reason, and, therefore, more immediate and spontaneous.

*Feedback*

After what we have experienced in this research into expression, we are in a position to verify if we are now able to:

* perceive the changes in our hands as they go through their movements;

* distinguish the relationship between these movements and our whole body, our whole person;

* distinguish the emotive changes brought about by these different movements;

* describe their active contribution to our experience, both day-to-day and out of the ordinary;

* pick out certain "words" better said with our hands than by mouth.

## EXERCISE 1

*Cup, or "willingness to accept"*

*Objectives*
(a) To come to appreciate that a hand, in the absence of contraction or extension, naturally takes on the shape of a "cup," a container.
(b) To come to know the symbolic meaning of the cup as *"capacity to accept."*

*Aim*
This exercise teaches us to express ourselves calmly.

We therefore let our body free itself from constrictions and emotional tensions.

Untensed, the body (and, here, the hands above all) takes on a concave position, as if waiting for a stimulus to summon it to movement, whether of closing in or of opening out.

Such a movement becomes indicative of a state of mind, of a willingness that we must learn to distinguish in our own experience.

From this emerges a form of expression which can be defined precisely as *"symbolic language,"* in that a particular gesture takes the place of a certain word which expresses a need or a state of mind or an attitude of the person **speaking him/herself**.

*Starting Position*
* Sit on your heels, or on the floor with your legs crossed.
* Rest your hands on your thighs, just above the knees, with the palms turned upward.
* Slowly bend your arms, resting them on the elbows, so that your hands come up towards your face.
* Stop when your arms form a right angle.

EXERCISE

* Look at your hands, picking out every last detail. You will see that, without the slightest effort on your part, they take the shape of a **cup**, into which anything could be placed without any danger of it falling out.

* Let your memory wander, so that it visualizes gestures from your past experience which can be recalled through the position your hands have taken on.

* You might perhaps see

– a beggar met at a street corner, or on the way into a church;

– a relative or friend asking you to do something to help them out of a difficulty;

– yourself at some dark moment when you looked for a gesture of solidarity from someone close to you . . . .

89

Basically, this **"hand-cup"** is simply asking to be filled with a **"gift."**

\* It is a declaration of our own capacity to see ourselves as "poor" just through the gesture of willingness to accept a "gift."
\* If we then join both hands together in the same expressive gesture, the image of the **cup** comes over with even more force.
\* **A cup, a glass, a container of any sort, show, in practice, a desire to be filled, to be completed.**

*Observations*
– It is interesting to note that when hands are held in this position, our whole body is drawn into a feeling of calm, of deep serenity, of relaxation.
– Furthermore, this is an excellent starting point for initiating any activity, whether negative or positive, of closing off or opening out.
– Muscular relaxation, the calm regularity of heartbeat and breathing, all form part of this symbolic language that expresses, precisely, **the capacity to accept any gift with serenity and respect**, even if the manner of "living with" this gift then becomes a matter of careful personal choice.
– Indeed, the characteristic of a **gift** is that it can be used according to the free will of the person who receives it. It is the recipient who can make it part of his/her experience, wholly or in part, who can even refuse it, wholly or in part, without feeling "conditioned" by the "mind" of the donor.

So, the characteristic of a gift is **risk in the way it is accepted**.
If a gift were to be accepted differently – respecting the wishes of the donor, that is – it would take on the aspect of

a *conditioning*, of *blackmail* even, of a *means of exchange*, of *money* with which to buy the *freedom* of the *poor* holding out their hands because they are in need.

We can therefore state that:
 – **each of us is a cup;**
 – therefore, **each of us needs to receive in order to be able to fulfil our basic nature;**
 – without forgetting, however, that **each of us has the right to be respected in our freedom to accept or refuse a gift.**

*Feedback*
\* The experiment carried out in this exercise has allowed us to observe the effects produced on our hands by taking up a position of calm: **absence of tension allows our hands to express an attitude of acceptance**.
\* Faced with our own experience or that of others, we are now able to read this position through the symbolic code of bodily language: **in order to able to accept, we, like our hands, must take the form of a receptacle, creating an inner hollow in which we can "hold other people as though they were gifts."**

**EXERCISE 2**
*Road, or "Capacity for Giving"*

*Objectives*
(a) To make ourselves conscious of the fact that our hands, given a certain *centrifugal* (from the inside out) tension of muscles and tendons, are constrained to open, to spread out, like a *table*, like a . . . *road*.
(b) To distinguish the symbolic significance of this table, this road, as **capacity to give, to open out to others**.

*Aim*
\* This is an exercise in observation and interiorization.

91

* It deals with hands that give, that do not hold back, hands that allow the gift we, in our turn, have indeed received, but have also changed into something new, something *personalized*, to slip into the cup of others.

* We sit at **table** for a limited time, as long as we need to share a gift we can enjoy together. We don't make the table our *base of operations*!

A **road** is a place of passage; it allows us to reach a goal. We don't make the road our *permanent dwelling-place*!

* **Table** and **road** together symbolize our desire and capacity to *communicate through giving*: to go out to meet others in order to fill their cups. This is the willingness to put the distributive capability we all possess into action. It is going beyond, overcoming selfishness and the mania for possessions. **It is sharing!**

* Therefore, this moving toward others, sitting at table with them, or walking down a stretch of road to meet them, expresses **movement, openness, life**: not a hardening of ideas, not a privatization and monopoly of gains we have made, not warning notices saying "Keep out: private property!" Rather: understanding that all we possess is the fruit of **contributions**, and, sometimes, sacrifices, made by others.

* Not a desire for security, but the capacity to **open out to others**, even when this means taking risks, in order to build a more genuine life.

* Not jealously guarding our own gains, but readiness to share the joys and troubles of a journey undertaken together.

* Not a wish to shut ourselves in by building a museum of gifts we have received, but the capacity to open our doors so as to appreciate these gifts in a play of continual interchange, in the wish that others too may share their advantages.

*Starting position*
– Sit back on your heels, or with your legs crossed.
Rest your hands on your thighs near your knees, palms facing up.
– Slowly bend your arms so your hands come up, till your arms form a right angle, hinged at the elbow.

EXERCISE
(a) Keep your hands relaxed, in the shape of a cup; recall all you experienced in the preceding exercise.
* Through your hands taking the form of a cup, your body was pervaded by a sense of wellbeing and of inner peace, expressed in muscular relaxation and in the calm regularity of heartbeat and breathing.

\* *Now, open your hands very slowly, till they are extended under tension to their maximum extent.*

All the muscles are brought into play.

Your breathing becomes deeper: the air going into your lungs can be better felt as sign of and potential for life.

Your blood is being pumped more forcefully into all parts of your body, impelled by a quickening heartbeat.

These are the results of a tension and an effort affecting your whole physique, and concentrated, precisely, in your hands.


(b) Now let us move on to *interiorize* the **significance** of this position.

\* **To communicate to another the gift I hold in my hands, I am required to make a gesture of active sharing, an effort**:

– I have to **move**, to let go, that is, of a security I had before, with the risk of losing the calm and tranquillity I had previously acquired, and go towards the other, about whom I know nothing or almost nothing.

But to do what?

– To **open my hands** and allow whatever I hold in them to go out, to slip into the other's hands, to go down the stretch of road between me and the other, and thereby fall into his/her cup.

\* This is the **symbolic language** of a gesture we repeat continually.

\* If this exercise is being carried out in a group, you can try out this movement of deliberately opening your hands concretely and visibly:

Suffice to let a little water or sand or any other object slip from your hands into the hands of those next to you.

\* It is important to look very carefully at all the movements made by your hands, and to notice how the rest of your body shares in their actions. And to perceive and experience the sensations and emotions that emerge at the level of the whole person.

*Observations*
– We are dealing with a language that forms part of our lives.
– The actual movements we make contain a symbolic language which it is important to interiorize in relation to our own experience.
– **It is our whole being that takes part** in the movement of opening our fingers so as to let our gift slip into another's hands.
– Giving something (a pencil, a book, a piece of bread – whatever) to someone implies:
* **capacity** to distinguish the demand or need expressed by the hands of another;
* **understanding** that we alone possess what can fill that other's hands;
* **realizing** the value we represent to that other at that moment;
* knowing how to **dispose** our will to the response;
* **moving** bravely away from the position of security we have learned to adopt;
* **going** towards another, even through the simple gesture made by one part of our body;
* **opening** our hands and allowing our gift to slip into another's hands;
* and, again, **accepting** that others will do with it what they will, in the light of their own real, actual situation.

We are easily led to think that gifts should, at all costs, be used in accordance with the intentions of the giver. This is a false assumption, arising from the fact that those who give are seen as rich and powerful by comparison with those who receive, who, in turn, are seen as poor and weak.

This assumption also normally conditions the relations between adults and children. The latter are seen as "empty vessels," to be filled, at all costs and by any means, with rules, laws, advice and regulations laid down by those who see themselves as guardians of the capacity to discern what is good and what is bad in their behaviour.

– This situation, seen from the child's point of view, easily leads to a vicious circle.
– In the long run, furthermore, it can help to produce a closed and defensive attitude: the child rejects an "imposed" gift and lacks the motivation to make "its own" gift to the other person as a means of communication.

We shall come back to this aspect in the next exercise.

*Feedback*
Looking back over the various stages of this exercise should show us that:
* the experiment we have carried out specifically indicates that our hands, subjected to centrifugal tension, **open and allow what is in them to fall out.** This movement also produces openness in the rest of our body, in muscular tension and in the rhythm of our heartbeat and breathing;
* **the symbolic language** expressed in the gesture of opening our hands denotes giving, the capacity to let go of our acquired certainties, to be able to share the products of our actions with others, even if this runs the risk of seeing them used in ways different from our intentions as giver.

**EXERCISE 3**
*Stone, or "Inability to Give or Receive"*

*Objectives*
(a) To take stock of the fact that, subject to *centripetal* (from the outside in) tension of muscles and tendons, our hands are forced to close into a fist like a **stone**.
(b) To distinguish the **symbolic meaning** of the stone, as a **refusal to communicate**, produced by closing-in on oneself, by self-absorption.

*Aim*
This exercise should show us that a **fist** is:
– **the closed hand of non-communication**, trying to keep everything back for itself;
– the hand ready to strike, because it is afraid that others will take away from it something it considers "its own," its "private property": it wants to keep all of this for itself, to defend it against the risk of its being turned into a gift;
– **the hand closed even to gifts** offered it by others, because it cannot admit its own limitations, or the fact that it needs others in order to grow, to reach its fullness;
– **the selfish hand that seeks to defend** all that it claims to possess through its own efforts, but does not in fact possess: What, after all, can a hand closed into a fist contain?

*Starting position*
– Sit back on your heels or with your legs crossed. Rest your hands on your thighs, by your knees, palms upward.
– Slowly bend your arms, allowing your hands to come upwards, till your elbows form a right angle.

97

EXERCISE
* If possible, use actual materials: your hands, cup-shaped, can be full of water or sand.

We are tired of this gift we hold in our hands, which we have made our own after having received it from another person.
* Next to us, someone else is holding out empty hands in the hope that we will pour our "gift" into them.
* At this point, we find so many difficulties developing inside us: if we respond, this is going to involve our whole being. We should like to give, but what we have is worth holding on to: it might well come in useful some time! And then will it really end there, or will the bond created between us lead us on to further risks, further requests, further denials?
* Meanwhile, the other person is waiting – hand held out to us, waiting only to be filled. It would be easy to satisfy this need, but, in the end, our dominant feeling is for possession, closing ourselves to and refusing the other person's request.
* There! Our hands close . . . . In the effort to retain what we possess and prevent this from becoming a "gift," **we contract our hands, as hard as we can**. Our whole body takes part in this contraction: it curls up into a ball. Our chest muscles stand out while our lungs are compressed by the curvature so that breathing becomes difficult.

We feel the heat rising to our face, feel it flushing red, while our veins swell and our heartbeat quickens.

We are filled with a feeling of unease, of **discomfort** in all our muscles, even in our bones, filling our whole being.

Nevertheless, we cling to our violent need to defend what we have and don't want to share with anyone else . . . at whatever price.
* Our fingers are curled tight, our hands closed into fists: they look like **stones** ready to strike out in order to defend, . . . anything rather than give!

*Observations*

– But . . . what can you defend in a closed hand? What can you hold in a tight fist? . . . water? . . . sand?

– A gift held back is distorted; it becomes something that even we cannot use . . . .

– We only have to open our hands to realize this unpleasant consequence of our selfishness: water, sand . . . the gift, is spilt. **Our hands are empty, seized up; they find it hard to regain their usual posture, their movement, their life.**

– The sense of unease resulting from this gradually returns our hands to a cup shape: the emptiness that pervades us simply reflects our need for other people and our desire for someone to *fill our cup,* to come to meet us in our poverty.

*Feedback*

Those who have carried out this experiment should be in a position to describe how their hands, subject to centripetal tension, produce a contraction phase in their whole body, forcing it to close in on itself, with resulting breathing difficulties, ending with it being forced to endure such discomfort that its means of communication are affected.

They should also be in a position to recognize the symbolic language expressed in this posture, as an indicator of **inability to communicate, of unwillingness** to share what we possess with others, or to accept from others what they would like to give us.

**This is the symbol of self-absorption, of egoism, of fear of taking risks.**

## 9
# PRAYING WITH OUR HANDS

### Preliminary Observations

* So far, I have tried to trace a possible path leading to examination, emergence and understanding of a linguistic code capable of demonstrating the symbolic depth of bodily expression, even if confined to our hands.

We have looked at this from a biblical and from a bodily standpoint, but to leave the matter there would be to fail in our purpose. We need to find a synthesis springing purely from our capacity specifically to translate an experience, an emotion, an outlook, into **prayer**: that is, into **personal communication with God**, using all our symbolic codes, including the **symbolic language of our body**.

* By carrying out the exercises proposed, we have come to realize that even the simplest gestures – a handshake, a glance, a smile – have the power to express, clearly and coherently, what we are and what we carry within us.

It is in this way that the **gestures we make with our hands** can become the expression of a genuine prayer, provided that we put our whole being, all our love, into them, and see them as a deliberate approach to the **Transcendent**.

* Physical expression in the area of communication allows us to realize its validity and importance as a way into

finding a proper and appropriate attitude to **prayer**.

\* The gestures we have found in the biblical quotations and examined in our anthropological research are "words" belonging to a **symbolic code** which is capable of communicating a deep message, full of meaning, because it is a human language, and therefore one that can be used **for human beings to communicate with God, in prayer**.


## The Expressive Gestures used by Human Hands in Prayer

Speaking of "hands in the language of the Bible," we had occasion to consider the symbolic force of their language in communication both between people and with God.

In our prayer too, especially in that of **the liturgy**, both public and private, our hands, like the rest of our body, take on a precise symbolic significance in relation to their position and movement. We probably do not always realize the significance these "words" take on in the context of our relationship with God. In fact, almost always, this significance does not depend on us, but on an anthropological factor that becomes charged with a new meaning precisely because one of the interlocutors in the dialogue is God.

Putting forward our selection of positions and explaining their meaning is not intended to close off other possible interpretations. It is simply one exposition, which can be modified and added to. Here, clearly, I am referring to a language that speaks in biblical categories, or in those used in the Christian liturgy.

### *Hands joined*
the position obtained by placing the palm of the left hand against that of the right, constitutes a gesture of
– **adoration**
– **inner turning toward God**
– **recognition of finding oneself in the presence of God.**

This gesture is usually accompanied by a forward inclination of the head, and made standing up with the upper body leaning slightly forward, as though to complement and accentuate the movement of the head.

### Hands open

in the shape of a cup, held together or apart from each other, and in front of the body, indicate a gesture of
– **acceptance**
– **willingness**
– **offering oneself**
– **offering a gift.**
This gesture can be accompanied or accentuated by the position of the body, standing or kneeling, in relation to the message being communicated: our face is either turned up, towards heaven, or down to our hands, to the gift:
*"Our hands open to you, Lord*
*to offer you the world . . . ."*

### Arms raised and hands stretched

is the gesture typical of the celebrant at the altar. It is also the gesture shown in the earliest images in Christian art as that of the *"orante"* (praying figure). This is understood as a gesture of
– **praise**
– **giving thanks**
and also of
– **asking** for a favour
– **supplication.**
In general, the body is held upright in a stance of openness, and the face turned upwards, to heaven, as though to indicate the transcendence of the One addressed.

## *Hands together with fingers intertwined*

and held against the breast, express
- **recollection**
- **interiorization**
- **quest for inner calm,** a parenthesis, a temporary shutting off from the reality around us.

Our body accompanies this gesture by collecting itself together: sitting or standing, our head is lowered forwards with our eyes closed. Our muscles are relaxed and our breathing calm and regular.

## *Hands and arms crossed on the chest*

are interpreted as a gesture of
- **assent** or
- **gratitude**.

In our culture, this gesture is found in iconography, particularly of the Annunciation. In general, it is made either standing or kneeling, accompanied by a slight inclination of the head and upper body.

## *Hands cradled*

one on top of the other, and open, in the Eastern manner, recall the image of the cup and express
- **meditation**
- **search**.

This is also a gesture of **acceptance**, in the sense of being willing to accept a gift, making oneself empty to allow it in. You can be seated, on your knees or standing up, with your eyes closed and your head slightly inclined.

## *Arms spread in the form of a cross, hands open*

are the intense expression of
- **prayer of intercession**
- **recognition of one's own powerlessness.**

You would generally be kneeling or standing, with your face raised to heaven or bent to earth, depending on the message you wish to express.

In **prostration**, this gesture serves as a visual accentuation of the expression of **nothingness**, with one's whole body pressed against the ground.

## Prayer in the Everyday Actions of Our Hands

We all have the capacity to choose and use attitudes and gestures suited to our own personality with which to communicate with the Transcendent. These gestures, then, possess the power to become *the words of liturgical language*, the celebration of the Way that God walks together with us.

Now, the examples and exercises given can provide a stimulus for a personal or group quest for similarities with other people who, like us, are expressing their own relationship with the God of Jesus Christ in the church community.

**Our hands, by reason of their symbolic language, indicate,** as we have said and seen, **human operativity, human action.**

We know, however, that we cannot close off the relationship we have opened up with God and confine it to the brief space-time we spend in prayer as such. **So this relationship, quite simply, occupies our whole daily existence, all human activity**.

Consequently, **prayer must reveal its full, multifacetted aspect and so bring the truth of its fruits to light**. The gospel exorts us to bring forth good fruit in all seasons – at every instant of our life, that is, and in all its expressions, by putting *the word we hear* **into action**:

*"Beware of false prophets: they come to you disguised as sheep, but inside they are wild wolves. You will recognize them by their fruits. Do you ever pick grapes from thorn bushes, or figs from thistles?*

105

*A good tree always yields good fruit, a rotten tree yields bad fruit. A good tree cannot produce bad fruit and a rotten tree cannot produce good fruit.* Any tree that does not bear good fruit is cut down and thrown in the fire. So you will recognize them by their fruit" (Matt. 7:15–20).